THE USBORNE BOOK

CASTLES

Lesley Sims

Designed by Ian McNee, Andrea Slane and Stephen Wright

Illustrated by Dominic Groebner,
Sally Holmes, Inklink-Firenze and Sergio

History consultant: Dr. Anne Millard

Edited by Jane Chisholm

Additional illustrations by David Cuzik, Ian Jackson and Justine Torode

Additional designs by Susie McCaffrey

Calligraphy by Tim Noad

Contents

The remains of Blarney Castle, near Cork in Ireland

astles & Internet links

While hundreds of castles across the world are falling down, new castle sites spring up almost daily on the Internet. Many of the more interesting castle Web sites have been suggested in this book. To visit them, go to the **Usborne Quicklinks Web site** at **www.usborne-quicklinks.com** and type the keywords "book of castles". You will find links which will take you to all of the sites, where, among other things, you can:

• Fire a trebuchet (a vast catapult) to end a siege

• Work out an escape route to rescue a prisoner from a castle dungeon

• Check out recipes for dishes that might have been eaten at a castle banquet

• Play a heraldry game identifying enemy knights by the coats-of-arms on their shields

• Take a virtual tour of Himeji-jo, a Japanese castle

• Use archery skills to save your life in a game set at the Tower of London in England

COMPUTER NOT ESSENTIAL
If you don't have access to the Internet, don't worry. This book is a complete, superb, self-contained reference book on its own.

Internet safety

When using the Internet, please make sure you follow these guidelines:

• Ask permission from your parent or guardian before you connect to the Internet

• If you write a message in a Web site guest book or on a Web site message board, do not include any personal information such as your full name, address or telephone number, and ask an adult before you give your e-mail address

• If a Web site asks you to log in or register by typing your name or e-mail address, ask permission from an adult first

• If you do receive e-mail from someone you don't know, tell an adult and do not reply to the e-mail

• Never arrange to meet anyone you have talked to on the Internet

Downloadable pictures

Pictures in this book marked with a ★ symbol can be downloaded from **Usborne Quicklinks** for your own personal use, for example, to illustrate a homework report or project. The pictures are the copyright of Usborne Publishing and may not be used for any commercial or profit-related purpose. To download a picture, go to **Usborne Quicklinks** and follow the instructions there.

Site availability

The links in **Usborne Quicklinks** are regularly reviewed and updated, but occasionally, you may get a message that a site is unavailable. This might be temporary, so try again later, or even the next day.

If any of the sites close down, we will, if possible, replace them with suitable alternatives, so you will always find an up-to-date list of sites in **Usborne Quicklinks**.

Notes for parents & guardians

The Web sites described in this book are regularly reviewed and the links in **Usborne Quicklinks** are updated. However, the content of a Web site may change at any time and Usborne Publishing is not responsible for the content on any Web site other than its own. We recommend that children are supervised while on the Internet, that they do not use Internet chat rooms, and that you use Internet filtering software to block unsuitable material. Please ensure that your children read and follow the safety guidelines printed on the left. For more information, see the "Net Help" area on the **Usborne Quicklinks Web site**.

🏰 **Internet links**

For links to suggested Web sites, go to **www.usborne-quicklinks.com** and type the keywords "book of castles".

Introduction

In which you can find
out what castles are and
why and when they were built.
You can also learn about
the earliest castles of all.

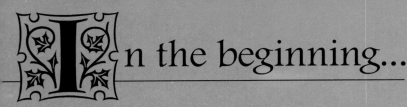n the beginning...

Europe a thousand years ago had no proper roads, no high-rise apartments, no sprawling cities. Instead, forests, marshes and farmland lay largely undisturbed, dotted with villages, small towns and castles. For 500 years, the castles dominated the countryside and their owners dominated the people.

What was a castle?

At its simplest, a castle was the private home of a lord or king, which was strengthened (or fortified) against attack. If it wasn't a home and a fortress, it wasn't a castle.

War with next door

The heyday of castles was in Europe between the 11th and 15th centuries, during a time known as the Middle Ages. Money and power were tied up in land. The more land you had, the richer and more powerful you became. People often didn't bother going to court to argue about rights either. If someone wanted more land, he simply took it – so wars between landowners were common.

Running to take cover during an attack

A castle let a lord dominate his own estates, while giving him a base from where he could launch raids on an enemy. It housed his family, his servants and soldiers, and was a place to retreat to in a crisis.

Choosing the site

Castles were often built at sites where rivers could be crossed, or at gaps in hills. Command of these key points helped castle owners control access to supplies and communications. This, after all, was a time when the closest thing to a mobile phone was a man on a horse.

Forts and castles

The idea of fortified homes wasn't new. Back in around 1800BC, the Ancient Egyptians built a string of forts in Nubia.

In about 1250BC, a fortified palace was built at Mycenae in Greece. It perched out of reach on a rocky outcrop.

People of the Iron Age lived in hill forts too. But these were all built for communities, whereas castles were for individual lords.

A license to build

The land on which castles were built came from the king or ruler. A lord never forgot this. He held his land on sufferance. If he upset his overlord, he lost it. Even building a castle was subject to the royal OK. Any lord wishing to crenellate (add battlements to) his home, was wise to ask his ruler first.

A noble asking his ruler's permission to build a castle

Striking the balance

Combining the dual role of home and fortress wasn't easy. It usually ended in uneven compromise. Early on in castle building, when wars with nearby estates were rife, lords depended heavily on defense. As the years went by and life was safer, they could pay more attention to comfort.

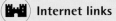 **Internet links**

Go to **www.usborne-quicklinks. com** for a link to a Web site where you will find a good introduction to castle terms with useful photos.

7

Castle times

When castles were first built, the Roman Empire, which held Europe together for hundreds of years, was a distant memory. Instead, Europe was a jumble of kingdoms, fighting each other for control. There were wars over land inside kingdoms too. With fighting all around, a castle was the safest place to be.

The feudal system

Most of the kingdoms operated what we know today as the feudal system. A king gave land to nobles, in return for their loyalty and help in war. The nobles gave land to knights, who fought for them. Knights gave land to villeins (peasants), who gave rent and other dues in return. Basically, you owed loyalty – and taxes – to whoever gave you land.

Some peasants owned their own land and owed no obligations. They were also free to travel where they wished – but they were few and far between.

Class rules

In the early Middle Ages, a person belonged to one of three groups: the ruling class of lords, who fought; the peasants, who worked; or the churchmen and women who prayed.

As people grew richer, a fourth class, of tradesmen, appeared. But at first, there was a place for everyone – and the feudal system kept everyone in it.

The feudal system in action

The ruler gave some of his land to nobles and high churchmen, who were his close supporters.

Channel hopping

Two kingdoms which had a special relationship in the Middle Ages were England and France. Thanks to royal marriages, English kings had land and castles in France – not to mention claims to the French throne. But the French kings would have none of it and attacked them constantly.

The nobles gave the king money and promised to fight for him for 40 days a year.

They gave some land to knights, who paid them 40 days' fighting service and other dues.

The knights gave land and their protection to the villeins.

The villeins farmed the land, paying their knight rent. They were "tied" to the land, which meant they couldn't leave their village to work elsewhere.

Social climbing

Inside a castle, people were very aware of their rank. The lord came top, with cleaners at the bottom. Everyone else was in between – with an eye out for ambitious underlings.

The lord's command

People came under one of several areas: the household, the estate, military or clerical (the Church). The lord was in charge of them all, but deputies ran things for him day to day.

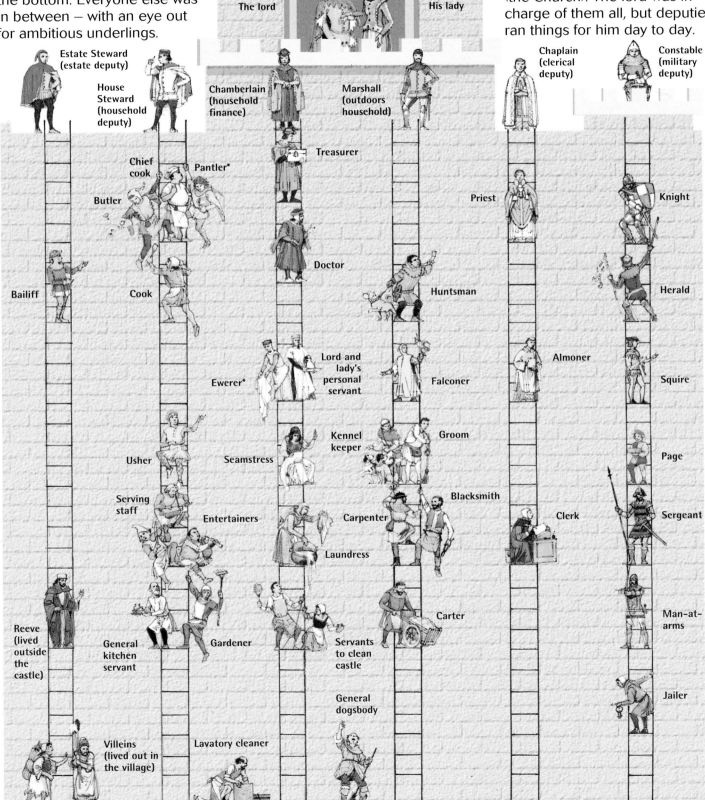

The lord

His lady

Estate Steward (estate deputy)

House Steward (household deputy)

Chamberlain (household finance)

Marshall (outdoors household)

Chaplain (clerical deputy)

Constable (military deputy)

Chief cook

Pantler*

Treasurer

Priest

Knight

Butler

Bailiff

Cook

Doctor

Huntsman

Herald

Ewerer*

Lord and lady's personal servant

Falconer

Almoner

Squire

Usher

Seamstress

Kennel keeper

Groom

Page

Serving staff

Blacksmith

Clerk

Sergeant

Entertainers

Carpenter

Laundress

Reeve (lived outside the castle)

General kitchen servant

Gardener

Carter

Man-at-arms

Servants to clean castle

General dogsbody

Jailer

Villeins (lived out in the village)

Lavatory cleaner

*You can find out more about the Pantler and Ewerer on page 70.

arly castles

Viking raiders attacking a village

The first castles, probably built in Europe before 950, were the result of an early insurance scheme. Villages were being terrorized by raiders, so lords offered to protect local villages in return for the villagers' land. They then put their soldiers on horseback, making a rapid response force which could race to villages under threat.

Since the soldiers needed a base, lords put up a wooden building to house them. This was protected by a ditch and a bailey – which was made up of an area called a ward, enclosed by a palisade (fence).

High on a hill

Of course, if the enemy burned down the palisade, the soldiers were left to fight to the death. The best bet was to build a keep, a secure building to be used as a last refuge. Ideally, the keep was sited on a hill, giving views of the country for miles around. If there wasn't a hill, a lord might have one built. The hill, or *motte* (from the Norman word for "turf"), could be linked to the bailey by a bridge.

Protect and serve

The spread of castles owed a lot to the rise of the feudal system. Once a noble had received his share of land from his ruler, he quickly erected a castle on it. The castle didn't only guard him from foreign invaders. It protected him from nearby lords with designs on his lands as well.

Roofs were thatched (covered in straw) and caught fire easily. An enemy attack with fire arrows was lethal.

These soldiers are racing from a motte and bailey castle to defend a village being attacked.

This bridge lifted up to secure the bailey when under attack.

Palisade of wooden stakes

Buildings inside the bailey included stables, workshops and often a chapel.

Main hall

Chapel

Ward

The bailey stood at the bottom of the motte.

William the castlebuilder

In 1066, William, Duke of Normandy, invaded England and claimed the crown. Wanting to show the Saxons who was boss and keep an eye on them in case they rebelled, he gave his supporters land taken from Saxon lords. Soon, Norman motte and bailey castles sprang up all over England. In less than two decades, 50 castles were built. They could be put up in a week and any buildings in their way were demolished.

A timber drawbridge linked the motte to the bailey. This could be partly drawn up when the castle was under attack, leaving a gap in the bridge.

The keep or "Great Tower"

The lord's family and servants could sleep here.

Stores and soldiers could be housed on the ground floor.

Guards patrolled the castle from this walkway, keeping an eye out for flares from villages under attack.

The palisade of pointed planks was about 2.5m (8ft) high.

The motte (earth mound) was difficult for attackers to climb at the best of times – and impossible in the rain.

Castles to go

Because they were needed in a hurry, timber for the castles was cut to size, packed with nails and pegs in barrels and sent over from Normandy. It was just like buying do-it-yourself furniture – with two differences. The Normans had a huge, if unwilling, Saxon workforce to assemble the castles, and there was no sending one back if two pegs and a plank were missing.

An inside passageway of Krak des Chevaliers, in Syria

Stone castles

In which you can take a whirlwind tour of castle history, seeing how castles changed after mottes and baileys. Then you can look at the developing castles in more detail, focusing on one or more of the rooms inside. Finally, compare photographs of different castles across Europe, before visiting a construction site to see how castles were built.

astles at a glance – part 1

The problem with castles which go up quickly is that they come down as fast. Any wooden keeps not burned by a rampaging enemy simply rotted where they stood. As early as 1070, a lord with the time, money and a suitable site, built in stone. These next pages show how stone castles developed.

Square keep

Early stone castles improved upon the idea of the motte and bailey keep. Rather than have the hall and lord's apartments standing separately in the bailey, the important buildings were piled on top of each other. A forebuilding was often stuck on the front, to guard the entrance. The result: a massive square keep which towered over the countryside, striking fear (or at least respect) into the hearts of all who saw it.

A Great Tower with one wall cut away

Walls could be up to 4m (13ft) thick.

Private rooms for the lord and his family were on the top floor.

The chapel

The Great Hall

The entrance was on the first floor to make it harder for attackers to get in.

A forebuilding guarded the entrance.

Stores and soldiers' quarters

Windows were small and high up for protection from enemy arrows.

With four floors, this is an example of a luxury square keep — many only had three.

Shell keep c.1100

Rather than build stone keeps, some lords chose instead to replace the wooden palisade with a stone wall, called a curtain. This type of castle was known as a shell keep.

A shell keep

Buildings stood against the curtain wall.

Chapel

Hall

Stores

Most shell keeps were circular, as here, but some were shaped like a four-leafed clover (*quatrefoil*).

Polygonal (many-sided) keeps
c.1150

But even stone keeps had their drawbacks. Archers could only see straight ahead through the windows, making the keeps difficult to defend. More seriously, the keep's corners could be undermined. Tunnels were dug underneath them so that they collapsed.

To tackle this, designers began to experiment with keeps of different shapes. Some had six sides, some eight. The designer of the keep below added four square towers to the main body of the keep, so there were even more corners – which rather defeated the object.

A polygonal keep showing the rooms inside

There were guard rooms at the top of each tower for soldiers to keep watch.

Upper Hall

Lower Hall

Kitchen

The chapel

Round keeps
c.1150

A variation on the many-sided keep was a keep with only one side: a round tower. This had no vulnerable corners to undermine, and missiles sheered off its smooth walls. Round towers also offered defenders a good range of fire.

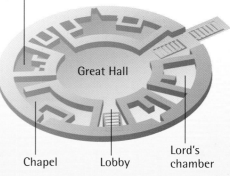

Latrine tower

Great Hall

Chapel   Lobby   Lord's chamber

Plan of a floor in a round tower

 **Internet links**

Go to www.usborne-quicklinks. com for a link to the Web site of an enthusiastic castle visitor. You can see photos of square keeps and polygonal towers. There is also lots more information (with pictures) on medieval buildings.

The Upper Hall was where the important members of the castle held banquets and entertained.

The Lower Hall was where the day to day running of the castle took place.

A small kitchen off the Lower Hall was used to reheat food cooked in the main kitchen in the bailey.

The lobby, with a prison cell beneath it. Most castles had a room to house short-stay villains.

Wall supports called buttresses

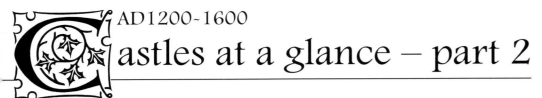

Castles at a glance – part 2

Despite the military advantages of round towers, most keep builders chose to follow the fashion of their area. Besides, there was a major drawback to all keeps, whatever their shape. Being dark, smoky, noisy and totally without privacy, they were no fun to live in.

Wall towers

If a castle's outer walls were strong enough, sometimes a keep wasn't even needed. Far more spacious accommodations could be built for a lord and his family in the bailey.

Towers known as "mural" towers were built into the wall, giving defenders extra places to fire weapons from. Soon, keeps both round and square, had fallen out of fashion.

Framlingham Castle in England had no fewer than 13 towers in its curtain wall.

Small garden for vegetables

Old Hall

Chapel

Soldiers' quarters

Well

New chapel and Hall

Kitchen

Gatehouse

Mural towers were built at regular intervals in the wall.

Gatehouse/barbican

As well as strengthening the curtain wall, the gatehouse at the entrance to the castle was fortified. Two wall towers were built close together on either side of the entrance, often with a room or two built between them on the first floor. A walled area was often left in front of the gatehouse as an extra defense. This type of heavily fortified gatehouse was known as a barbican.

A barbican

Guardrooms were on the ground floor of the towers.

A portcullis (iron gate which could be raised and lowered) guarded the entrance.

Rooms for the castle Constable were in the towers.

Barbican tower

Concentric castles c.1280

In the late 13th century, castle designers introduced a new style into Europe – concentric castles. Named after their rings of walls, concentric castles were often more regular in shape than earlier castles. Their designers also used water defenses wherever possible.

The idea possibly came from the Land Wall in Constantinople (Istanbul). Built in the fifth century AD, it was actually three walls of decreasing height. Archers on the upper walls could shoot over the heads of soldiers below.

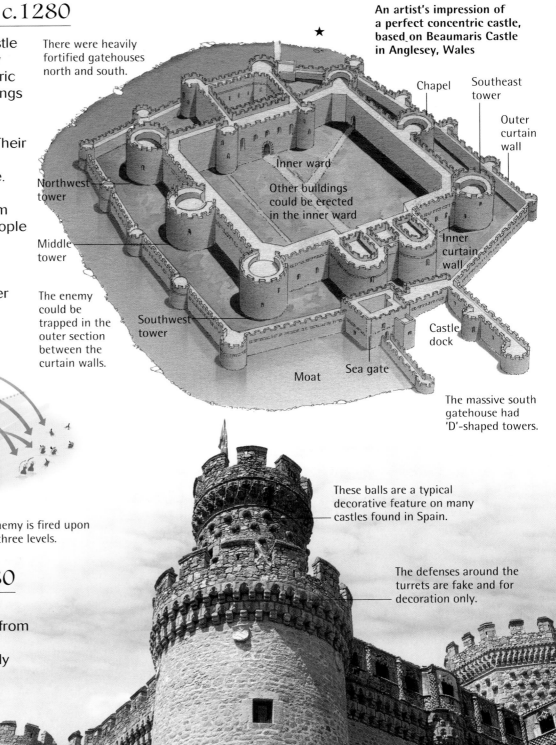

★ **An artist's impression of a perfect concentric castle, based on Beaumaris Castle in Anglesey, Wales**

There were heavily fortified gatehouses north and south.

Chapel

Southeast tower

Outer curtain wall

Inner ward

Other buildings could be erected in the inner ward

Northwest tower

Middle tower

Inner curtain wall

The enemy could be trapped in the outer section between the curtain walls.

Southwest tower

Castle dock

Moat

Sea gate

The massive south gatehouse had 'D'-shaped towers.

A concentric castle, designed for attack as well as defense

The enemy is fired upon from three levels.

These balls are a typical decorative feature on many castles found in Spain.

The defenses around the turrets are fake and for decoration only.

Later castles c.1380

By the late 14th century, castles finally moved away from the "defense first, comfort nowhere" motto, which early designers took to heart. Instead, they became lavish homes.

El Real de Manzanares Castle in Spain

El Real de Manzanares is an example of a castle-palace: solidly built but with more comfortable living quarters.

Only one room really counted inside a square keep: the Great Hall. From the very beginning, it was at the heart of castle life. The Hall was where people ate, worked, prayed, slept and, in the early days, even cooked.

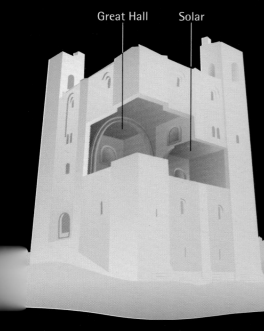

Great Hall   Solar

Not only was it a focal point where people in the castle met to eat and socialize, it was an audience chamber for outside visitors and became a courtroom whenever the lord had to judge local disputes.

Decor

Above all, the Great Hall was the castle's showpiece, where a lord could show off his wealth. Stonework was elaborately carved. Ceiling beams were edged in gold. Vast tapestries covered the walls — partly to brighten the place up, though mostly to cut out drafts — and dozens of candles lit shadowy corners. But Great Halls were still dark, if not downright uncomfortable. With footsteps clattering on stone stairs and doors banging shut, they were also very noisy.

The solar

Most keeps had a solar, a private room for the lord and his family. This was just off the Hall or, occasionally, on the floor above. The solar was both family bedroom and sitting room for the lady. The lord relaxed there too, when he wasn't off somewhere giving orders.

Solars were often decorated with wall paintings, like this one of a saint from the Pope's palace in Avignon.

A day in the life of the Hall

As there was no electric light, people were up at dawn to make the most of the daylight. After prayers, tables were laid out for breakfast — usually a simple meal of bread and ale.

Then the tables were put away and castle business took over. The Hall became an office apart from a break mid-morning — for the main meal of the day — when it was a dining room again.

Supper was at sunset, then the Hall became a dormitory. If you were important, you had your own room (though your servants came in with you). Anyone else bedded down in the Hall.

The upper level window balcony let people watch the action in the Hall and keep an eye outside too.

Wall hangings were huge.

A window seat was one of the few places in a square keep for a private talk.

The lord's coat of arms

A man-at-arms

The Bailiff listening to a reeve

The House Steward

The lord is listening to an angry tenant, with his Estate Steward sitting on his right.

The man by the dog is a clerk and he's supposed to be making notes.

Setting up the first of the dinner tables

An open fire in the Hall was the main source of heat.

Rushes covered the floor

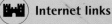 **Internet links**

Go to **www.usborne-quicklinks.com** for a link to a Web site with excellent close-up photos and a model reconstruction of Rochester Castle in England (one of the oldest square keeps in Britain).

 Square keeps & the kitchen

Castle kitchens were a huge problem. Apart from the smells and smoke, there was always a risk of the floor rushes going up in flames. To avoid the kitchen setting light to his entire castle, a lord had it built as far away from other buildings as possible.

But, as food quickly cooled on the long walk between the bailey and Great Hall, this meant a succession of cold dinners. So, some castles had a second – much smaller – kitchen off the Great Hall, just used for reheating food.

A castle kitchen preparing for a banquet

Mass catering

Many lords owned more than one castle and shared their time between them. When the castle was only occupied by the Constable and soldiers, it was busy enough. But when the lord and his entourage (not to mention visitors) were in residence, the kitchen – and staff – were frantic. Cooking vast meals, and often banquets, for up to two hundred diners, took blazing fires, scores of servants and a great deal of shouting.

A woodcut of cooks preparing and tasting food

Pots and pans

Swinging over the fire were the cauldrons, heavy iron pots which were vital pieces of kitchen equipment. Peasants made do with one, sealing food in separate bags and cooking everything together. But castle cooks had a variety – large pots for soups and stews, smaller ones for sauces. Most utensils were made from iron too. Bowls were generally earthenware or pewter, though wealthy lords ensured their families and guests dined off silver and gold.

Carrying in a deer

Baking bread

Cauldrons

Food on a spit

The "turnspit"

Plucking a goose

Bringing water from the well

The pantry

The name for the pantry or larder, the domain of the Pantler, came from French. Originally, it was known as the *paneterie*, where *pain* or bread was kept.

The buttery

It sounds like a dairy store but the buttery, under command of the Butler, was where the beer and wine were stored. The name came from *bouteilles*, the French for "bottles".

Wine would have been served in a ewer like this one.

Running water

Fresh water (or as fresh as it got), came from a well linked to an underground spring. A well was safest actually in the castle, since one of the first ploys of a besieging army was to poison the water supply. The job of fetching and carrying water belonged to a kitchen servant called a scullion.

The cellar

Since kitchens didn't have refrigerators or freezers, the coldest place to keep food was the cellar. With no preservatives either, food was salted, smoked, dried or pickled to make it last.

Spices were valuable and locked away.

The brewhouse

Beside the kitchen was the brewhouse where ale (weak beer) was brewed. Made from oats, wheat, barley and water, it was the staple drink – so it was useful that the brewing process sterilized the water.

Dried herbs

Arise Sir Chef!

Good cooks were highly prized. One lord was so pleased with his chef that he made him a knight. The knight didn't forget his origins. He had three cooking pots added to the design on his shield.

The tomb of the chef knight shows him in battle dress with his shield.

★

Chief cook

Marzipan castle

Sugar cones

🏰 **Internet links**

Go to **www.usborne-quicklinks. com** for a link to a Web site where you can learn more about medieval cookery. There are six galleries of pictures (click on "A Feast for the Eyes"), and even an authentic recipe for medieval gingerbread.

from c.AD1100
Shell keeps & the chapel

A lord with a working castle, who wanted to jump on the stone bandwagon, simply replaced his wooden palisade with a stone curtain wall. Some lords thought a wall was enough defense in itself. Rather than build a tower keep too, they put up a stone wall with buildings against it, making a shell keep.

A shell keep

The chapel(s)

The plan of a shell keep on the right highlights one of the most important rooms in any castle: the chapel. Few castles had torture chambers, but every castle had at least one chapel, in the keep or bailey. Some castles had both: a private one for the family and a more spacious but less grand chapel for the household. However religious you were – and everyone was, to some degree – you were expected to attend church on Sunday. Many people went daily, though as the service was sung in Latin, it mostly went over their heads.

A ground-floor plan of a shell keep

Store room · Chapel · Guard room · Ante-chamber · Courtyard · Small hall · The Great Hall · Gateway · Kitchen

Going to church was seen as a way to get into heaven. Soldiers, certainly, might not have spent much of the day praying. But you can be sure if a battle was looming, or they were in trouble with the Constable, they'd be in the chapel, having a chat with God.

Inside a castle chapel

Stained glass windows were only used after 1350.

Scenes from the Bible were painted on the walls.

Chalices like this were used in church for Communion.

The altar

The altar boy

Priest saying mass

The lord and his family

Many people saw church as the chance to gossip.

There were no pews. If you were too old to stand, you brought your own seat.

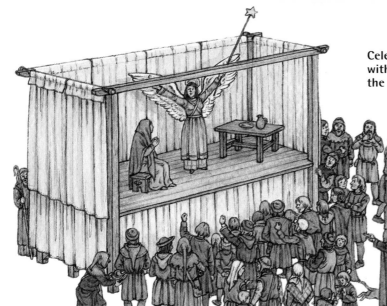

Celebrating a holy day with a performance of the Nativity

 **Internet links**

Go to **www.usborne-quicklinks.com** for a link to a Web site which plays Gregorian chant (traditional medieval church music which was named after Pope Gregory I).

Dancing in the street

The chaplain trying to get people to watch the play

An almoner giving food to the poor

The chaplain

The man in charge of religious life in the castle was the chaplain. He took all the church services and said a short prayer before every meal. But, as one of the few people in the castle who could read and write, he also took charge of the castle records, supervised clerks and helped to run the lord's estate. Some chaplains even found time to teach the pages to read and write. (Pages were nobles' sons who were training to be knights.*)

The almoner

Religion was all about living a good life. If you wanted to be a good Christian, so the chaplain would preach, you had to offer charity. Most castles had an almoner who ensured that alms (money) and leftover food were given to the poor.

Charity was crucial in the Middle Ages, since there were neither insurance policies nor government benefits to apply for. The poor, sick and disabled had to rely on charity – or starve.

"Holydays"

Most people in the castle probably enjoyed their holy days the most. These were the original holidays – religious festivals when everyone was given the day off. To keep the religious theme, actors would perform plays based on the Bible, or act out scenes from the lives of saints.

Pilgrims

Some people also went on long pilgrimages (trips to holy sites) to please God. If there was no inn nearby, pilgrims passing through a village might turn up at the castle looking for a bed for the night.

This medieval painting shows pilgrims setting off to prove their worthiness to God.

* See page 69

Outbuildings

As well as the really significant rooms (whether in a keep or the bailey), castles had many other buildings for their on-site support teams. In fact, most of castle life took place in the bailey. Some servants may never have gone inside a keep at all, unless the lord took pity on them during a siege.

Plan of a castle showing the outbuildings

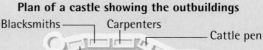

Blacksmiths — Carpenters — Cattle pen — Mews — Fletcher — Keep — Chapel — Stables — Wall tower — Bailey — Well — Great Hall — Soldiers' quarters — Kennels — Kitchen

Blacksmith

A skilled blacksmith was one of the lord's most important servants. In modern terms, he was a mechanic, combat-gear manufacturer and tool maker rolled into one.

Not only did a specialized blacksmith, called a farrier, shoe the horses, blacksmiths made and repaired all of the other workmen's tools. The smiths also had the vital task of repairing the lord's (and his knights') battle armor.

Inside the smithy

Fletcher

The blacksmith made the metal tips of arrows (medieval bullets), while a fletcher made the flight (end feathers) and wooden shaft. An expert bowman might not have had automatic machine gun fire, but he could still fire off an arrow every few seconds.

Casting arrow heads

Fire

Anvil

An apprentice melting iron in the fire

The farrier, making a horseshoe

The lord

Repairing a rivet on the lord's knee plate

The fletcher's hut

An apprentice being shown how to fix feathers to a shaft

Carpenters' workshop

Carving a bowl

Carpenter

A man in constant demand was the carpenter. Since there was no plastic, he didn't just make and repair furniture, but bowls and tool handles too. He also repaired wheels, built frames for shields and patched ceiling beams and floorboards.

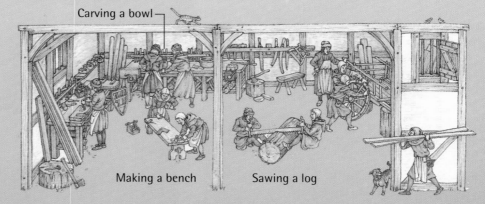

Making a bench

Sawing a log

The stables

Stables

The main means of travel was horse power and the stables housed horses for every occasion. Top of the neighing order were destriers, the lord's war horses. Next came palfreys, for his everyday riding, and coursers for when he hunted.

Women, who didn't fight and rarely hunted, could ride palfreys or hackneys. Then came packhorses to carry baggage and, finally, carthorses to pull the wagons.

Tacking up

A farrier cleaning out a horse's hoof

Unloading a packhorse

A lord setting off on his destrier to improve his skills with a lance (wooden spear)

Hawking on a hackney

A squire trying to rein in his unruly palfrey

Mews

A mews today might house homes for the rich. In the Middle Ages, it was where the falcons lived.

Giving the birds some air. Falcons were sprayed with water to calm them down.

Birds of prey such as falcons were used to hunt small animals and birds. They were trained and cared for by a falconer and his assistants.*

* See page 78

Kennels

Dogs were kept both as pets and for the most popular of medieval pastimes: the hunt. Hunting wasn't merely sport, but a way to provide fresh meat for the castle's larder in winter.

Because of this, hunting hounds were kept in luxury in the castle kennels. They were often better fed, and usually more comfortable, than the kennel boys looking after them.

A huntsman taking the dogs for a walk

These are breeds you don't see today.

There were several different dog breeds. The lymer sniffed out prey; the others chased it.

Levrier

Levrier

Lymer

Brachet

The lady's lap dog

f an enemy got into the bailey, a lord's days were numbered. Eventually, the keep would fall. The trick was to keep the enemy out in the first place. So, heavily fortified gatehouses were built at the castle's weakest point: the entrance.

The guardrooms

Taking up most of the space inside gatehouse towers were rooms for the Constable (the man in charge of castle security), and the soldiers.

The first gatehouses had just one tower. An enemy at the gate could only be fired on from above.

★

The soldiers spent most of their time off duty hanging out in the guardrooms on the ground and first floors. When on duty, apart from guarding the castle, they patrolled the lord's estate and searched all incoming deliveries.

Days were broke drills, archery and while they waited Dice games and f maids helped pas on the whole it wa

A gatehouse with the away to show life insi

The Constable's solar

Soldiers passed the time playing games and chatting.

Guardroom

For extra safety, there was no access to the upper rooms from rooms on the ground floor.

Pikes

The Constable

Usually in charge of the castle in the owner's absence, the Constable was responsible for all military personnel. His main job was to defend the castle and be ready for attacks. He did this by making sure the buildings – and soldiers – were prepared. He also rounded up any knights who owed the lord 40 days' fighting service.

The jailer

If the Constable was head of security, at the bottom, literally, was the castle jailer. Most castles had cells for the few prisoners they housed at any one time. These were mostly local villains awaiting trial on grave charges such as murder or serious assault.

On the whole, though, castle prisoners were nobles: either knights who'd been captured in battle or, occasionally, political prisoners (who held views which angered the lord or threatened the king). They were kept in guest rooms and generally well-treated. With the knights, there was always the hope that a handsome ransom would be paid for their release.

Internet links

Go to **www.usborne-quicklinks. com** for a link to a Web site with a castle to explore. If you visit Bleak Tower in the castle, and creep past Harold the Jailer, you'll find a prisoner in the dungeon who needs help to escape.

Dungeons

"Dungeon" comes from the Norman word for keep: *donjon*. No one knows for sure why the word changed to mean a prison underground. Some medieval prisons did look very like keeps. Also, castle keeps were so secure, they were the obvious place to hold prisoners (though not always in the darkest depths).

Two prisoners taken from a medieval manuscript

The rarest prison cell was the *oubliette* – from the French, meaning "to forget". Because of this, people think it was somewhere you were thrown and forgotten about until you died. But prisoners were tried – and sometimes executed – never forgotten. It really meant that the outside world forgot about the prisoner.

Inside the cell of a peasant prisoner

A caring family would bribe the jailer to allow extra food and blankets for a prisoner.

Prisoners were fed a diet of bread and water.

Manacles were used to chain a prisoner's feet together.

Bucket for slops

from c.AD1270
Concentric castles & more rooms

Not content with wall towers and fortified gatehouses, lords wanted stronger castles still. They found them in concentric castles. These worked on a "walls within walls" system. While ideal for defenders, for attackers they spelled disaster. Once past the first wall, they were trapped. With defenders behind and in front, they had nowhere to hide.

★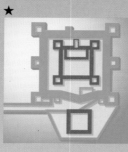

Belvoir Castle, Israel

★

Caerphilly Castle, Wales

★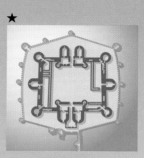

Beaumaris Castle, Wales

Gilbert de Clare, the Norman lord who built Caerphilly Castle

King of the castle

Caerphilly Castle in Wales was the first concentric castle in Britain. It so impressed Edward I he used it as a blueprint for four of his castles in Wales. Today, Harlech, Aberystwyth, Rhuddlan and Beaumaris are among the best-known concentric castles in Europe.

Built from 1277 to 1330, the castles were huge, costing the king a fortune. Apart from sheer size, they're unusual because each castle was planned and built all at once. Most other castles were simply altered each time a new trend came along.

Last but not least

Beaumaris Castle on Anglesey in Wales was the last, some say best, of the bunch. It's an unfinished example (even kings run out of money), of the perfect concentric castle. Work began in 1295, continuing on and off for 30 years, before stopping for good in 1330. Designed to be impenetrable, it was never put to the test – though its size may have made would-be attackers think twice.

Caerphilly Castle in Wales is surrounded by a vast artificial lake, which was created by damming a river.

Changing times

Concentric castles are often declared the high-point of military design. But though defense was paramount, 13th century designers were starting to take living quarters into account. Extra towers in the extra walls made room for more rooms and privacy at last. It was a far cry from sleeping squashed up in the Great Hall and whispering secrets in window seats. Servants no longer had to share rooms with their masters (just each other).

The bathroom

By the 13th century, one room was noticeable by its absence: the bathroom. People did take baths but it was a nuisance carrying hot water up from the kitchen. Instead, they threw herbs around to hide the smell. Toilets, or garderobes, were simply set into the wall, often in rows. A few early castles had basic running water systems and washbasins – but usually only for the kitchen dishes.

Suites of rooms were built for guests, where a visiting lord could stay with his entourage.

Rooms for important guests had wash basins built into the wall.

Just off the bedroom was the closet, a dressing room used to store clothes, and the bathtub when not in use.

The garderobe was simply a stone seat with a hole in it, hidden by a curtain.

The servants' quarters were much more basic.

Garderobes emptied straight into the moat or a pit called a cesspool.

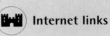

Internet links

Go to **www.usborne-quicklinks. com** and enter the keywords "book of castles" for links to the following Web sites:
Web site 1 Find out more about Welsh castles
Web site 2 See close-up photos of Caerphilly's defenses in an on-line picture gallery
Web site 3 Take a virtual tour of the Tower of London, which was converted into a concentric castle

c.AD1350~1500
Later castles

At the same time as demanding castles with maximum defense, by 1350 some lords were looking for more comfort in their living quarters. For the first time, the design of the residential side became as important as the military.

A lord now wanted a status symbol that was a comfortable home. As the threat of attack grew less, windows were enlarged, lifting the gloom, and many were glazed. The fanciest ones had stained glass. Fancier still, the newest castles were built from brick, not stone, with room for any number of guests.

Bodiam Castle

Bodiam Castle, built in England in 1385, had spacious, carefully planned accommodations. There was even room to separate the lord's quarters from his servants' — probably to make it harder for outside attackers to reach him.

Stained glass was colorful and intricate, as shown by this detail from a window in Alcazar Castle, Segovia, Spain.

Keep out!

Lords living in newer castles had begun to appreciate the privacy extra space could give. In the later castles, they really spread out. Now, lords had a separate room for each activity, including rooms just to hold court or bathe in.

It was something Frederick I might have appreciated. While meeting nobles in Erfurt Castle in 1184, he popped into the garderobe. The nobles, wanting to continue their private chat, trailed after him. The garderobe floor collapsed and several lords ended up in the cess pit.

The magnificently painted bathroom of Pope Clement VII in Castel Sant'Angelo, Rome

Plan of Bodiam Castle, Sussex, England

Southeast tower / Southwest tower

★

Ante room / Great Hall / Pantry / Buttery / Kitchen

Hall / Servants' hall

Chamber / Servants' kitchen

Chapel

Household apartments

Northeast tower / Gatehouse with guardrooms / Northwest tower

Home improvements

Every aspect of home life was more luxurious. Fireplaces became grander, dominating walls. Newly introduced chimneys drew the smoke away. Early castles had made do with smoke vents and the smoke billowed back into the rooms.

Furniture was intricately carved – and there was far more of it. Any wooden beams were highlighted with gold paint. Woven mats replaced floor rushes and, in the grandest of castles, Persian carpets sat on the mats. The first of these carpets may have been brought back as gifts by knights who fought in the crusades.

House and garden

The enthusiasm for doing up the castle inside spread to the bailey. Soon, formally laid out gardens were springing up, complete with fountains and garden seats.

The royal bathroom in Leeds Castle, England

Linen was draped over the wooden bathtub to avoid splinters in the royal bottom.

Table manners

The more civilized surroundings brought with them a new etiquette (way of doing things). Tablecloths replaced bare boards on every table and forks were used to eat with for the first time. Handkerchiefs were used for the first time too – at the table and elsewhere.

An early 14th century silver-gilt casket used to store precious objects. Even storage became more elaborate as people rushed to fill their castles with magnificent items.

This German model, of St. George slaying a dragon, is an aquamanile – a water container used to wash diners' hands at the table.

 **Internet links**

Go to **www.usborne-quicklinks. com** for a link to a Web site with a detailed history of Bodiam Castle, plus photographs of the outside and the ruined interior.

ariations on a theme

The important thing to realize about castles is that no two castles are alike. The basic design was endlessly adapted to suit where a castle was built, when it was built, whether the lord paying for it had new-fangled ideas, and how rich he was. As trends changed, early castles were often drastically altered and enlarged, becoming a mishmash of styles.

All shapes and sizes

A castle's style often depended on the region in which it was built. Because part of Spain was once ruled by Muslim Moors, and then Christians, Spanish castles combine the styles of both. La Mota (below) is the perfect example. It began life as a Moorish castle and then had several alterations before the Christians carried out major works in the mid-15th century.

La Mota, a brick–built castle in Spain

No ladder or wooden tower could be built high enough to reach the tallest tower.

The falconer's castle

Frederick II, the Holy Roman Emperor, had his castle, Castel del Monte, built around an eight-sided courtyard. As the Emperor had a passion for falconry and hunting, the castle was probably a hunting lodge.

Castel del Monte in Italy, begun c.1240

Plan of Castel del Monte, showing the access to Frederick II's apartments

Each of the castle's eight towers also has eight sides.

The view from inside Castel del Monte looking up to the sky

Arrow loop*

The decorative brickwork on the outside is in the Moorish style.

Gun loop*

* See page 45

Towering above

A simpler, cheaper alternative to a full-blown castle was the pele tower. This was a miniature version of a square keep. Pele towers were built on the border between England and Scotland. Some didn't even have steps at their entrances, simply a ladder or rope up to the first floor.

Larger than pele towers were tower houses, built in Ireland after the 1400s and in Scotland a century earlier. The Scottish tower houses weren't only defensive on the outside. Inside, they were set up for spies.

Channels called "luggies" ran between two rooms — so a conversation in one could be overheard in the other. Some tower owners went further, building hidden staircases and false floors to confuse intruders.

Chillon Castle stands on an island in Lake Geneva in Switzerland. This style of castle, with roofs capping each tower, is typical of castles in continental Europe.

Craigievar, a Scottish tower house

Craigievar is a massive seven floors high.

An attack of Wartburg Castle, in Germany, taken from a medieval manuscript

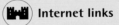

Internet links

Go to **www.usborne-quicklinks. com** for links to the following Web sites:
Web site 1 Find out more about pele towers and tower houses
Web site 2 See photographs of French and Belgian castles
Web site 3 Explore a photo gallery with pictures of European castles including some in Germany, Britain, Ireland and Scandinavia

AD1150-1250
Building a castle

Whatever the style, when a lord wanted a new castle, his first step was to appoint a Master Mason. Also known as the Master of Works, the Master Mason was chief architect, surveyor, project manager and accountant. With him on board, the lord sat back and opened his treasury. (Castle building was an expensive business.)

Choosing a site

The next step was choosing the site. Castles were positioned to guard frontiers, ports, cities and important river crossings. They had to be well-placed for attack and defense and be in a good position for managing the lord's estates. There were also more practical questions to ask:

* Where's the nearest water supply?

* Who owns the closest wood and quarry?

* Can any stone be quarried on site?

* Is there a nearby river so materials can be sent by boat?

and, finally,

* Where will all of the workmen come from?

Starting work

Before the castle went up, carpenters built lodges for the craftsmen and a tracing house with a plaster floor, on which masons drew pillars and windows to calculate their measurements.

Inside, walls were a cobbled together mixture of rubble, flint and old brick.

The scaffolding poles left gaps in the walls called "putlog" holes.

"Putlog" hole

Digging a ditch for the moat

Building work in progress – building a castle took hundreds of people

Stonemasons cut and shaped stones to fit on site.

Wooden scaffolding was made by the carpenters.

Winter break

Unless the castle was a rush job, work stopped for winter. The tops of the walls were covered in straw to protect them from frost.

Heaving stones into place

A lodge

Mixing mortar

A treadwheel was used to lift heavy items. It was worked by two men from the inside (like hamsters in a wheel).

Wooden frames were used to support arches while they were being built.

The lord discussing plans with the Master Mason

Carts, sleds and wheelbarrows were used to transport materials.

For the outside walls, ashlar (cut stone) gave a smooth finish.

onstruction workers

When building a castle, the wage bill was one of the biggest costs. The Master Mason was no average earner himself. One of the most famous, Master James of St. George, earned five times more than anyone else. But when you consider the sheer number of people he had to organize, you realize he was worth every penny.

Extract from a letter sent from Master James to the royal treasury in February 1296

In case you should wonder where so much money would go in a week, we would have you know that we [need] 400 masons... 2,000... workmen... 200 quarrymen [and] 30 smiths and carpenters...

A mason's tools of the trade

Dividers, for measuring and marking out stones

A mallet (left) and chisel (below), used for chipping out stone

Masons

Masons in their hundreds worked in stone. There were two grades: freemasons cut and shaped the ashlar and other, more decorative, stones; roughmasons (laying masons) laid the stones in the walls.

This is meant to be a cathedral for Charlemagne built in the 8th century – but the artist has set it in his own time, several hundred years later.

Each roughmason had a symbol which he used to sign his work. This wasn't a matter of pride but a way to prove how much he'd done, so he'd be paid.

A roughmason's symbol

A medieval artist's impression of builders at work

Carpenters

Even on stone castles, carpenters were kept busy. All the scaffolding was made of wood, for a start. Then there were wooden defenses, floors, ceilings, inside panelling, doors and shutters – not to mention the furniture. To reflect the carpenters' importance, on many projects the Master Carpenter was second in command to the Master Mason.

A carpenter's adze (right), for shaping and smoothing wood

Smiths

Smiths were the crucial metal workers, who made tools for the carpenters and masons (not to mention themselves). They also made door hinges, and nails by the thousand to hold floor, door and ceiling planks together.

A blacksmith's snips (for cutting metal)

General workers

Unlike the craftsmen, who sometimes came from all over Europe, the general workers on a building site were drawn from surrounding villages. They had the heavy work: mixing cement by hand, digging trenches for foundations and dragging stones into position. It was seasonal work too. Unless the castle was needed urgently, when the winter came they were laid off until spring.

Quarrymen

Where possible, a castle was sited relatively close to a good supply of stones. Often, though, stones were ordered either from the other end of the country or from elsewhere in Europe. In that case, quarrymen cut them roughly into shape before loading them onto a boat, for the river or sea journey to the building site.

Hauling up a bucket of plaster using a rope and pulley

Internet links

Go to **www.usborne-quicklinks. com** for a link to a Web site about cathedrals, where you can learn more about masons and medieval building techniques.

Plasterers & painters

Castles were highly decorated both inside and out. Even where the finest stone — or even marble — was used, it was considered unfinished if left unpainted. Outside walls were often coated in whitewash. Inside, walls were painted with bright geometric patterns, wildlife or religious scenes.

Plasterers and painters putting the finishing touches to pillars and walls in the Great Hall of a square keep

Decorative carving at the top of a pillar

Smoothing plaster on the walls

A wooden scaffolding tower

The Master Mason giving instructions

Outline of the pattern being painted

A fierce battle scene from a medieval illustration

War

In which you can see a full range of weapons and armor and learn the tricks of castle defense. You can witness a siege at its height and find out how to capture and defend a castle, before visiting the famous warrior castles of the crusaders and the samurai.

c.AD900~1500
Choose your weapon

Which weapons you used depended on whether you were a knight or a footsoldier, and whether you were fighting a battle or defending a castle. In battle, knights fought with lances and expensive swords, which were as much a status symbol as a weapon. Soldiers on foot used spears, pikes and bows. But when defending a castle, the weapon of choice was the crossbow. Introduced in the 1100s, it was thought so lethal, two Popes tried to ban it.

Bows and arrows

Archers, using longbows and arrows, were given a grudging respect by knights on account of their numerous victories on famous battlefields including Crécy and Agincourt. The early Norman bow was relatively small and with a small range of fire. The longbow, developed in the 1200s, was a much larger weapon.

A barbed arrowhead called a "broadhead"

A pointed "bodkin" arrow

Arrows had wooden shafts of aspen or ash, and goose feathers in their flights.

Unlike the Norman bow and longbow, the crossbow fired bolts. It also took time to fire, unleashing only two bolts a minute. But, though it took a while to reload, this could be done in safety behind the battlements — and if a bolt hit its target squarely, no armor could protect the victim.

Flight

Longbow

Pikes and spears

The most basic weapons were spears and the even longer pikes. Both could cause horrific injuries. Knights were often unable to break through rank upon rank of pike-wielding footsoldiers en masse.

Using a longbow took great strength, but a fit bowman could fire off up to 12 arrows a minute. Almost as tall as the archer who fired it, the longbow sent arrows almost 300m (1,000ft). So, captured archers had their fingers lopped off to prevent them from firing more bows. This gave rise to the "V" sign, a taunt to the enemy that they were still able to let loose arrows.

Crossbow and bolt

Early crossbows were operated by brawn; later ones (like the one above) used winches.

Axes, maces & flails

Up on their warhorses, knights used battle axes, maces and flails. These could strike a lethal blow against plate armor. A flail was swung around the head and used to pull an opponent from his horse.

Pikes could be up to 5.5m (18ft) long.

Spears were nearly 3m (9ft) long.

A "flanged" mace

A halberd — a type of ax

A flail

The mace was like a club with a heavy metal head.

The spiked iron ball on a flail could catch on a knight's armor.

Swordplay

Swords were extremely heavy, their blades endlessly worked on by swordsmiths to strengthen them. Early swords had a double cutting edge but later ones had a sharper point. This helped them to slip between plates of armor, piercing the leather jerkins – and flesh – beneath.

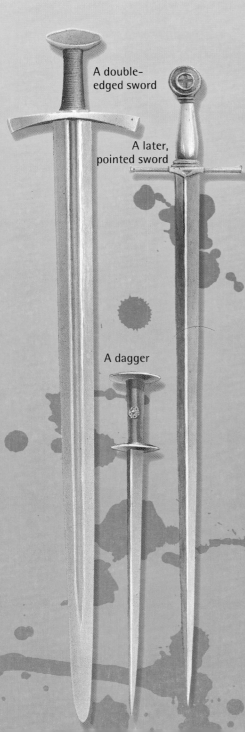

A double-edged sword

A later, pointed sword

A dagger

Gunpowder plot

Gunpowder was known in China by the 1st century AD, but it wasn't until the 14th century that it had any impact in Europe. In 1330, the Italians invented "thunder tubes": metal tubes welded together through which gunpowder was fired.

At first, accidents were common. Even 100 years after thunder tubes, or cannons, were invented, James II of Scotland was killed when one exploded. But designers were continually improving them. By the 1500s, cannons could fire balls long distances, with devastating effects, blasting holes in the strongest of walls.

Swords for hire

Technically, all knights owed their lord or king 40 days' fighting service. But, if the king wanted to wage a campaign overseas, it could take much longer. In this case, the king took cash from his knights and hired mercenaries (professional soldiers).

The solution worked well in war time, but left disgruntled soldiers in times of peace. They went on the rampage and generally made nuisances of themselves. Eventually kings realized it would be best all around if they had a paid army.

Firing an early cannon

A statue of an Italian mercenary, known as a condottiere

All wrapped up

The development of arms and armor went hand in hand (or gauntlet in gauntlet). As arms grew more lethal, armor had to offer more protection. Knights in early castles wore a simple chainmail tunic called a hauberk (made of iron rings linked together). By 1200, this had become a suit, with mail leggings and mittens.

Underneath his hauberk, a knight wore a gambeson (padded jacket), or a lighter version called an aketon. This protected him from blows and also stopped the chainmail from rubbing his skin raw. But chainmail only gave limited protection. A direct hit from a lance or arrow was fatal.

Outfit of early 13th century chainmail

A long tunic called a surcoat was worn over the hauberk to deflect the sun. It sometimes bore a knight's coat of arms.

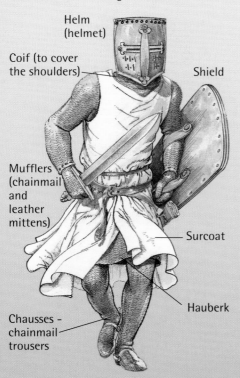

Helm (helmet)

Coif (to cover the shoulders)

Shield

Mufflers (chainmail and leather mittens)

Surcoat

Hauberk

Chausses - chainmail trousers

Plate armor

The next stage came in the 14th century, when steel plates were used to cover parts of the body. These were jointed, so knights could still swing their swords, axes or flails with ease. Gradually, the plates were joined together. By the 1400s, they made a suit. Surprisingly, this was no heavier than the chainmail suits of previous centuries. Because the weight was spread over the body, not hung from the shoulders, it may even have felt lighter.

Head start

Norman helmet

A square helm

An engraved basinet with lift-up visor

Early knights wore a pointed metal cap with a nose guard, on top of a chainmail hood. A century and many injuries later, the nose guards were wider and the hats had become rounded. Some decades after that, the helm was introduced: a square helmet which covered the entire head. But its eyeslits gave a very narrow view of the battlefield. Soon, helms were put aside for the basinet, a helmet with a "pig-faced" visor, so-called because of its shape.

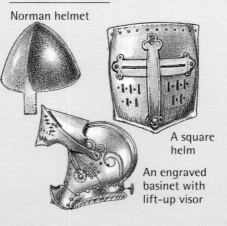

Helm

Pauldron (plate for shoulders)

A 14th century suit with the beginnings of plate armor

Couter (elbow plate)

Gauntlet (glove)

Many knights wore a coat of plates (a tunic with leather or metal plates sewn onto it) over their hauberks.

Poleyns (protected the knees)

Spur

Cover story

With armor expanding to cover the whole body, shields could get smaller. A knight relying solely on chainmail needed a shield almost as big as he was, to hide behind. But a 15th century knight was so hidden by his suit of armor, he could throw his shield away.

Shields through the ages

Early Norman shields were huge.

Over time, shields developed a distinctive base-of-an-iron shape.

Finally, they became merely decorative.

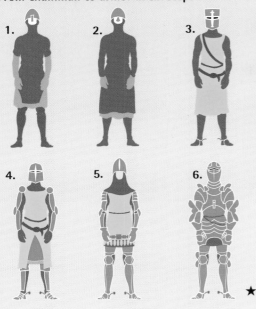

From chainmail to armor in six steps

1.
2.
3.
4.
5.
6. ★

Key to armor

- Chainmail
- Padded jacket
- Wool leggings
- Surcoat
- Leather belt
- Coat of plates
- Plate armor
- Metal belt

A 15th century suit of armor worn by Duke Siegmund of Austria

Suits followed fashion. Some lords even had pleats in their armor.

This spike was used to rest a lance on

Breastplate

Gauntlets were jointed so fingers could move

Cuisse

Greave

Armor like this was difficult to walk in – but that's because it was designed to be worn on horseback.

Off the peg or designer?

As the demand for armor grew, an industry grew with it. This was mass-production on a massive scale. An army might order 3,000 helmets and 5,000 new aketons, though footsoldiers often made do with used armor.

For themselves, lords ordered custom-made suits. The best came from armor-producing families in Germany or northern Italy, such as the Missaglias. Their armor had fans all over Europe. Suits came stamped with the family emblem, which led to forged marks and a lucrative trade in imitation suits.

Some lords even outfitted their horses in armor, though this was rare because it was so expensive.

A lord and his horse in custom-made suits, ready for battle ★

Castle defenses

Over the years, designers grew ingenious at finding ways to protect a castle. Natural features, such as cliffs, were used to make approach next to impossible. Walls were built over 4m (13ft) thick to prevent destruction by a battering ram.

Top-of-the-range castles had many other hurdles too. (But the theory that stairs turned to the right to give a descending, sword-wielding defender the advantage, is probably a myth.)

Mottes and moats

Because weapons had a short range of fire, the best defense was to stop the enemy from getting near the castle in the first place. So, if there was no convenient cliff, you made a hill (motte) to put your castle on and surrounded it with a ditch or moat, ideally filled with water.

Bridges

To cross the moat, you needed a bridge. Swimming wasn't an option in armor — and it wouldn't have been much fun doing the crawl through sewage.

Less hi-tech castles had a fixed bridge, but most of them had moving ones, which could be whipped up when the castle was under attack.

The designers of Alcazar, a castle in Segovia in Spain, used the natural defenses to their advantage.

Moving bridges

One of two moving bridges could be attached to the front of a gatehouse: a lifting one, or a turning one.

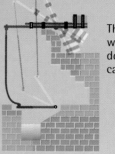 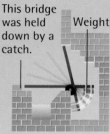

This bridge was held down by a catch.

Weight

The lifting bridge   **The turning bridge**

Gatehouse

Once over the bridge, you reached the entrance. Until the arrival of fortified gatehouses, this was the castle's weakest link. The gatehouse enclosed a passage which had two more defense systems: the portcullis and murder holes.

The portcullis was a gate of wood and iron bars which was winched up and down to let people in and out.

Murderholes, or meutrières, were holes in the roof above the gate passage, used to throw down stones on the enemy or water to put out fires.

Battlements

At the top of every wall were the battlements or crenellations, built with crenels (gaps) and merlons (solid sections) at regular intervals. These gave the archers space to fire their arrows and something to shelter behind while they reloaded.

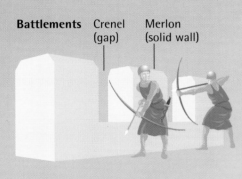

Battlements   Crenel (gap)   Merlon (solid wall)

Firing loops

Inside the castle, defenders shot through loops (slits) in the walls. These had to give as wide a view of the outside as possible, while being too small for enemy missiles to get in.

This archer has to fire his bow through a fairly narrow arrow loop. Later loops were designed with angled sides, which gave castle defenders more room to fire.

When bows were replaced with guns and cannons, gun loops were built into castle walls, with a hole at the bottom for the gun.

Looking like an upside-down keyhole, a gun loop was also known as a keyhole gunport, or oilette.

Hoardings

To give a better range of fire over the enemy, timber extensions called hoardings were built around towers and along the walls. These often had roofs, and gaps in the floor, allowing soldiers to bombard the enemy with missiles. But hoardings caught fire easily and could be quickly smashed to pieces by rocks.

A battering ram was used on the corner of a tower to knock down the wall.

Animal skins soaked in water protected the ram from "pots of fire" (jars filled with flaming rags).

Some towers were built on angled bases. Missiles dropped from above bounced off the castle onto the attackers.

A castle under attack

A "pot of fire"

Climbing up to attack the hoardings

Machicolations

Because of their vulnerability, over time wooden hoardings were rebuilt in stone. These were known as machicolated parapets, from "machicolation", the name for the gap in the stone floor.

Throwing rocks down on attackers through the machicolations

An extending ladder, used to reach the battlements – if the soldiers can fix it in place

Under siege

From the French *siège* meaning "a seat", a siege is literally where both sides sit it out. It's the last resort of a desperate enemy, as sieges cost huge amounts of time and money. With castles designed to be impenetrable, you may wonder why they were attacked at all.

There were two reasons. First, capturing a castle gave a lord control of all the land that went with it. Secondly, if he skirted around a castle to an easier fight ahead, he left an enemy behind him, who could launch raids from the rear and destroy his communication lines.

The siege season

The best time of year for a siege was late summer, ideally before the harvest. This meant crops to feed the besieging troops were still growing in the fields. Any later risked the fall rains, which would mean a wash-out.

But whichever time of year they attacked, plotting armies used every trick in the book to try and defeat the home team. There were usually advantages and disadvantages on both sides. Over the next four pages, their game plans, tactics and siege weaponry are considered in detail.

This scene shows a siege at its height. Unless a lord was spectacularly unlucky, not everything shown here would happen at the same time.

A mangonel (like a giant catapult) flinging large rocks toward the castle

A priest giving a soldier the Last Rites

At the front of this tower, a ramp is lowered to let the enemy soldiers onto the battlements.

A counterweight trebuchet (see next pages) hurling a rock at a section of castle wall

Attackers used giant shields to get closer to the castle.

The leader of the enemy plots a strategy by his tent.

Some of the soldiers on the battlements are stuffed dummies – to make the enemy think the castle is more heavily defended than it is.

Lowering a grappling hook: with luck, it will trap the head of the battering ram before it can do much damage.

Scaling ladder

A maid rushing out with more arrows

A mattress cushioned blows from a ram.

Battering ram

Nifty forkwork will topple a scaling ladder with several soldiers on it.

The enemy filled in the moat with dirt and wood, so their siege engines could be wheeled up to the walls.

Capturing a castle

An attacking army's most useful weapon was surprise. Catch a castle unaware and a siege could be over before it had begun. Even during a siege, if the castle soldiers let down their guard for one minute, the enemy would sneak in. Besiegers also tried bribing someone on the inside to let them in.

If surprise didn't work, the next stage was direct assault. At its simplest, some of the attackers scaled walls with ladders, while others fired flaming arrows to cover them. When climbing failed, war machines called siege engines were constructed. These had to be wheeled up to the castle walls, so the moat was filled in first.

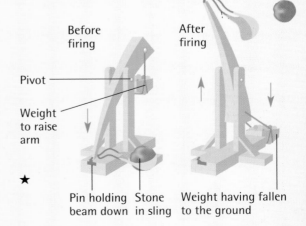

A siege tower up against the wall of a besieged castle

A drawbridge at the top of the tower gave access to the battlements.

Attackers were protected inside the tower.

Siege engines

The most basic siege engine was a belfry (tower), used to gain access to the battlements. But this was notoriously unstable, often toppling over on the uneven ground. For destruction, you needed a ram or giant catapult. Both blasted a hole in a castle wall. The ram, being hand-held (by dozens of hands), was easier to aim. But the two weapons based on the catapult, the mangonel and trebuchet, were more deadly.

The mangonel, based on a Roman catapult, was basically a giant spoon containing a missile. It was held down by ropes and then released.

★

Twisted ropes

The trebuchet, developed from the mangonel, was far more powerful and accurate. Trebuchet operators were highly skilled, able to hit the same patch of wall time and again, to weaken and destroy it.

A modern reconstruction of a trebuchet

Arm on a pivot

Net for the missile, whether rocks or dead animals (which spread disease)

Before firing

After firing

Pivot

Weight to raise arm

★

Pin holding beam down

Stone in sling

Weight having fallen to the ground

Flies and mud pies

You might think an attacking army held all the cards. If the heavy artillery failed, they simply had to wait until the castle's food ran out. But that could take months and, in the meantime, the castle could be organizing help from outside. The besiegers also had to feed themselves. Stolen crops didn't last forever and, besides, the thefts angered the locals.

If it rained, an army found itself encamped in a sea of mud on an already basic campsite. With no toilets, dysentery and cholera ran rampant – along with the flies. Disease and gangrene from infected wounds laid soldiers low much more effectively than weapons.

A lord could keep some men besieging the castle and send others ahead, but it weakened his force. And those left behind faced unending boredom as the weeks became months. Bored soldiers fought among themselves. They also grew sloppy, making it easier for those inside the castle to sneak out and launch surprise attacks.

Inside a knight's tent, a doctor treats the wounded.

A rain-lashed camp

Internet links

Go to www.usborne-quicklinks.com for a link to a Web site where you can fire an animated trebuchet. You'll need to decide various things, such as how close to go to the enemy castle (too close and you're shot), and how heavy your missile should be. You can also see photographs taken of a group of researchers as they built and fired their own trebuchet.

Undermining

A really sneaky enemy didn't knock down walls at all. He tried to come in underneath them. Mining soldiers (often called sappers), built a tunnel up to the castle walls. The tunnel was held up by wooden props which were then set alight. The resulting blaze caused the tunnel to collapse, bringing down part of the castle with it.

In 1215, King John of England undermined the power of a rebel baron at Rochester by digging under a corner tower of his keep. The fire in the tunnel was kept going with the fat of 40 pigs, until the tower (and the baron) caved in.

Building a tunnel up to a tower to undermine a castle

Hauling up the rubble

Rubble from the tunnel could be used to fill in the moat.

Wooden props supported the tunnel.

Footsoldiers did the heavy work of digging and bringing out the stone.

efending a castle

When the worst happened, and an army set up camp outside his walls, the first thing a lord did was to try to get a message to a local ally for help. Then he began rationing food and kept an eye on the water. (Castles would fall if an enemy poisoned the water supply.)

Picking up a stray soldier with the "crow", a giant hook

Dirty trick

A besieged castle even needed soldiers on lavatory watch. King John lost Chateau Gaillard, his castle in France, in 1204 when a very brave French soldier (possibly with no sense of smell) crawled up the garderobe chute. He arrived in a castle lavatory, climbed out and let in the others through a window.

Sorties

Attack being the best form of defense, sorties (surprise raids) were vital. These usually took place at night. A small group of soldiers would creep out by the postern, a side gate hidden by bushes. With luck, they caught the enemy off guard and could set light to their camp, or destroy a siege engine before it was fired.

The advance troops wait to be let into the castle.

Direct action

From inside the castle, archers kept up a constant barrage of arrows onto the besiegers. Other soldiers fired red-hot rocks or sand, and men-at-arms used long forks to push scaling ladders away from walls. They even used an enormous device known as the "crow" to hook up enemy soldiers who strayed too close to the castle walls.

Men took turns to watch from the gatehouse, armed with boiling water to pour through the murder holes in its roof. In an early attempt at germ warfare, rotting carcasses were fired into the castle. These had to be burned before they spread disease.

The garderobe

Sneaking into a castle via the garderobe chute

Sewage flowed straight into the moat.

Tactics

While attacking a castle took hordes of men, defending one could be done with a handful. At Caernarvon Castle in 1403, 428 men withstood a siege in which their attackers lost 300. Putting dummies on towers was a good way of fooling the enemy into thinking they faced a garrison of hundreds. Pelting the enemy with bread also implied food was plentiful and the castle could last for a year.

Mines test

Bowls of water were placed on the floor around the castle to test for tunneling. Ripples on the water's surface meant the enemy was probably digging underfoot. Men were put to work at once on a counter-tunnel. They tried to meet in the middle, where they could fight it out underground.

Surrender?

Apart from starvation, and disease, the biggest problems were boredom and lack of contact with the outside world. The enemy cut off supply lines and caused confusion by spreading false stories.

If the castle inhabitants gave way to panic, they could always agree on a date for surrender if help hadn't arrived. Knowing the siege wasn't indefinite tended to put the enemy in a friendlier mood. So, even though a lord ended up losing his castle, he (generally) didn't also lose his life.

Trebuchet Express

Even if surrender was in the cards, it was very important not to send out a herald to parley (discuss it), unless a lord was sure his attacker was ready to talk. If he wasn't, the herald would probably return via trebuchet: head first, body later.

Tricks & spies

Any chance to break a siege had to be grabbed. When the Empress Matilda was besieged in Oxford Castle in winter 1142, she dressed in white and fled across the frozen moat, hidden by the snow. In another siege, a spy discovered the besiegers all ate at the same time. The castle soldiers rushed out and caught 140 men as they were eating.

Tricks worked both ways. In 1341, Sir William Douglas re-took Edinburgh castle by disguising himself and some friends as peasants laden with supplies. As soon as the castle gate opened, they held it open with their carts, rushed in and massacred the garrison before the soldiers were fully awake.

Secret passages were often built into castles to get escape parties out and supplies in. But, if they found the passages, attackers could get in through them too.

Attacking soldiers in the mine about to face the besieged enemy in their countermine

Countermine

Putting up props

Mine

A castle soldier listens for sounds of the enemy digging, to see how close their tunnel is.

Internet links

Go to **www.usborne-quicklinks. com** for a link to a Web site where you can find out more about siege tactics.

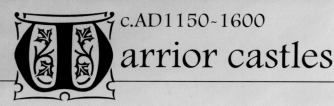 Warrior castles

Castles were built all the way across Europe into western Russia, but this wasn't the only part of the world to need heavily defended castles. When the crusaders journeyed to the Middle East in the 11th and 12th centuries, they found Muslim strongholds so impressive they took them over – and built new ones too. Three hundred years later, while European lords turned from defense to comfort, powerful warlords in Japan were building castles of their own.

Krak (or Crac) des Chevaliers, a concentric castle in Syria, was rebuilt by crusaders on the site of an earlier Islamic castle.

Crusaders' castles

The first plea to crusade (go on a holy war) came from Pope Urban II in 1096, when he called for European knights to go on a crusade to win back Palestine from its new Muslim Turk rulers. Thousands of knights responded.

Many may have been inspired by religious zeal, but the thought of glory and wealth probably clinched it. Along the way, the knights built castle bases to guard their route. From these, they could launch attacks on nearby towns.

A Middle Eastern city under siege

If time or the place were against them, they quickly built a plain enclosure, with towers set in strong walls, surrounded by a ditch. Ideally, they chose inaccessible spots, high on cliffs, or the opposite, right in the middle of busy trade routes.

Kerak Castle in Jordan was sited for maximum disruption to the Muslim line of communication. It suffered constant attacks until, in 1188, the Muslim ruler Saladin finally captured it.

Overhanging roof

Japanese castles were built on slopes to make access harder.

The rocks in the base were joined together without cement.

 Internet links

Go to **www.usborne-quicklinks. com** for a link to the following Web sites:
Web site 1 Take a virtual tour of the labyrinthine Himeji-jo (unlike earlier invaders, you get a map)
Web site 2 Take a more in-depth look at Japanese castles (with dozens of photographs)
Web site 3 See pictures of Krak (called "Crac" here) des Chevaliers

Jo and the warlord

Japanese lords, known as *daimyo*, built castles partly to protect their families and soldiers, but also to show how rich and powerful they were. The castles are named after their site, followed by *jo*, the Japanese for castle.

Early castles were simple lookout towers on mountains. But these were remote, hard to fight from, and impractical for large armies. So, "tower-castles" were brought down from the mountains and built on hills.

Since, being lower, they were easier to attack, hill castles were built with moats, walls, watch towers and two-stage gates to trap attackers. The tower became larger and formed the central *istenshu* or keep. It was set in at least three baileys, laid out like a maze to confuse invaders. Before their castles were built, the *daimyo* laid out ropes in the shape of the design, to make sure it worked.

The main tower is 46.4m (153ft) high.

A Japanese knight called a samurai. His armor is made of plates which are lacquered to keep them from rusting.

Japanese knights

Several thousand miles from Europe, the Japanese had independently developed their own feudal system. Central to this were *samurai*, knights who were fiercely loyal to their lord and fought for him, often in return for land. *Samurai* warriors upheld a strict code of chivalry, which stressed bravery and decency.

Himeji-jo, a hill castle in Himeji, Japan, nicknamed "the White Heron"

The upper levels were wooden, plastered to protect them from fire.

Japanese castles had machicolations too, called *ishi-otoshi* (rock chutes).

The central tower housed the lord and his family. Servants and soldiers lived in buildings around it.

Rock chute

A medieval illustration of a tournament in full swing

The age of chivalry

In which you can read about knights
and the rise of chivalry and see
a tournament taking place.
You can also trace the development
of heraldry and learn how to interpret
coats of arms.

Knights & chivalry

If you wanted to be a knight, having a wealthy father helped. A knight wasn't simply a soldier on horseback. He had a high social position to maintain and a knight's life was expensive. Not only would he have to pay for all his horses, weapons and men, he was expected to give his friends generous gifts.

For a young boy, the route to knighthood was to become a page and then a squire. Occasionally, squires were knighted on the battlefield, but knighting usually took place, with great ceremony, in a castle.

From squire to knight in 6 easy steps

1. The night before the big day, have a bath. Don't forget to scrub behind your ears. (Knights are clean.)

2. Go to the castle chapel and spend the night praying that you will be a good and worthy knight.

3. Get dressed in your finery, helped by a page and another squire. Allow enough time. It's quite a performance.

4. Kneel before the lord for your "dubbing" which makes you a knight. It's a tap on the neck so don't move!

5. Remember to thank the lord as he presents you with your own sword and spurs.

6. Go back to the chapel for the castle priest to bless you, so you will always triumph in battle.

A knight ready for the battlefield, from an illustrated Italian manuscript

Knight life

Most knights held land from a lord in return for 40 days' military service, dividing their time between home and the lord's castle. When they weren't guarding the lord, or fighting for him on a campaign, they toured the tournament circuit for extra money.

Support staff

Knights rarely went anywhere alone. Along with his pages and squires, fighting men, servants and equipment, a knight also needed at least three horses: a war horse for battle; a palfrey for travel; and a pack-horse to carry all the luggage.

A knight with his servants and horses on the move

Chivalry

Originally, if you were chivalrous, it meant you were good on a horse. (The word "chivalry" comes from *cheval*, the French word for horse.) But by the 12th century, chivalry was a code of conduct for knights. They had to be kind, truthful, loyal, polite to women (including their sisters) and noble in battle. It was a lot to live up to – and many didn't.

Troubadours

Chivalry was encouraged by troubadours, who were knight-minstrels. They wrote songs, not just about knights doing heroic deeds, but knights who did them for the love of a woman. This love was pure and noble and required above all that knights respect women.

It was quite a change for women, who'd previously been treated as part of the furniture. Taking their lead from Eleanor of Aquitaine, a queen of France and England in the 12th century, women welcomed troubadours and their ideals into their homes.

St. George and the princess, a popular chivalrous tale, painted on a wall of San Zeno Maggiore, a church in Verona, Italy

Internet links

Go to **www.usborne-quicklinks. com** for links to the following Web sites:
Web site 1 Learn more about knights on a site by students – you'll find lots of written information and a couple of good photographs of armor
Web site 2 Rescue a knight in the game "Rescue at the Castle" where Sir Crispin is being held prisoner...

The lady of the castle listens to news from her lady-in-waiting's letter, ignoring the knight serenading her.

c.AD1100~1450
Tournaments

If there was no local war to keep a knight fit and his skills up to scratch, the next best thing was a tournament: pounding hooves, clashing iron, the roar of the crowd – and a chance to win some money into the bargain.

Tournaments grew out of the French *melée* (or "free-for-all") of the 11th century. This was a full-scale, fake battle. But the resulting injuries and deaths were all too real, so the *melée* was condemned by the Church and replaced by more organized forms of combat.

Knights waiting their turn at the tilt

The joust

Once *melées* were strictly controlled, they became less popular. Instead, people were gripped by the joust: two knights on horseback and a head-on collision course. The goal was to charge and unseat your rival using a lance (a long spear). Knights could break up to three lances. After that, they fought with swords on foot, until one knight was forced to his knees or dropped his sword.

A tournament around 1350 in full swing

Horses were protected with armor and straw padding.

A lance

This vanquished knight is desperately trying to buy back his horse and spurs.

Profit and loss

By the 13th century, chivalry was in fashion, and tournaments became even more civilized. No longer a war but a pageant, knights came from all over the country to take part. Though they no longer risked their lives, they risked losing everything else. The defeated knight had to give the winner his horse and armor – or hand over its equivalent in cash. Terrible injuries were also common.

Tilting at targets

By the 15th century, jousting knights thundered along either side of a long wooden fence or "tilt". It worked on the same principle as a highway barrier to keep the knights apart.

A thief

The tilt was introduced because so many unseated knights were trampled to death by their opponent's horse.

The host's coat of arms

A page climbing the stand to get a better view

A herald announcing competitors

Tents of visiting knights

The winner's cup

A stretcher party carrying off an injured knight

The Lord and Lady, their guests and important townspeople watched the jousting from decorated stands.

The tips of lances were blunted but there were still horrible accidents.

This area was known as the tiltyard.

The tilt

One of the lord's guards

Selling hot pies

Sideshows

Many tournaments also provided wrestling bouts, archery competitions and sword fights. The whole day was a major social event. It gave the nobles a chance to put on their finery and gave the peasants a break from the fields.

An archery competition taking place

Heraldry & coats of arms

One knight in a helmet looks very much like the next, so knights painted designs (or arms) on their shields to identify each other. They also put arms on their tunics, or surcoats, which became coats of arms.

A coat of arms

Today, the phrase "coat of arms" refers specifically to the arms themselves, which are always set in a shield. Shields are divided into sections, to make it easier to describe the coats of arms. (If "left" and "right" appear to be on the wrong side, imagine you're holding the shield.)

The background, called the "field", can be painted as a metal: silver (*argent*) or gold (*or*); as a color: blue (*azure*), red (*gules*), black (*sable*), green (*vert*) or purple (*purpure*); or painted to look like fur, such as ermine.

The different sections of a shield

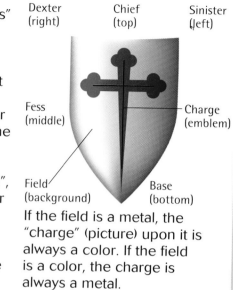

Dexter (right)   Chief (top)   Sinister (left)

Fess (middle)

Charge (emblem)

Field (background)   Base (bottom)

If the field is a metal, the "charge" (picture) upon it is always a color. If the field is a color, the charge is always a metal.

Arms were especially useful at tournaments, run and scored by heralds. The heralds, who introduced each knight as he rode out, soon became expert arms spotters. It was a short step from recognizing coats of arms, to recording them and designing new ones – a system which became known as heraldry after the heralds.

This image, part of a stained glass window, shows the Emperor Rudolph I with his coat of arms.

Family arms

Nobles handed their coats of arms down the generations and plastered them over everything. Most girls used their fathers' until they married, when their family arms were joined with those of their husbands. Boys had their own, a variation of the family arms, depending where in the family they came.

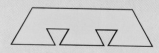

While his father was alive, an eldest son's arms bore this symbol, called a "label".

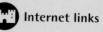 **Internet links**

Go to **www.usborne-quicklinks. com** for a link to a Web site where you can play a heraldry game, spotting enemies by their shields. There is quite a lot to read but it gives a good feel of life in the Middle Ages.

A spotter's guide to arms

Heralds recorded all designs on rolls of parchment. The simplest designs are known as "ordinaries":

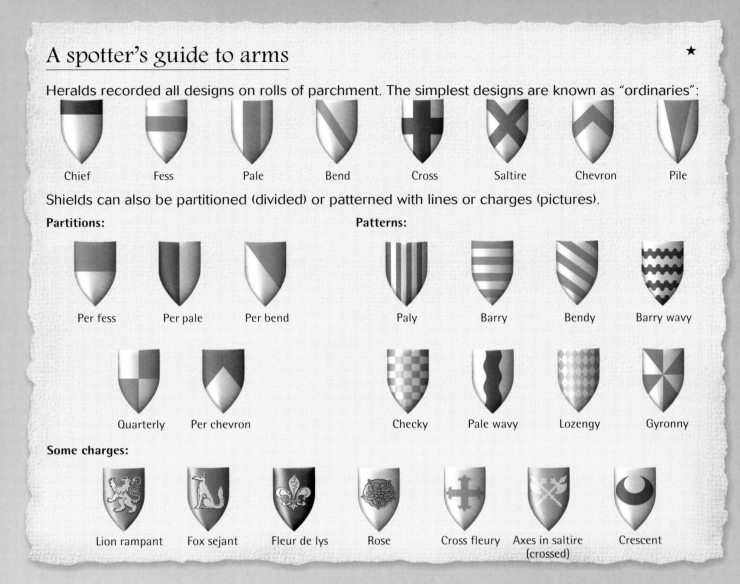

Chief   Fess   Pale   Bend   Cross   Saltire   Chevron   Pile

Shields can also be partitioned (divided) or patterned with lines or charges (pictures).

Partitions: **Patterns:**

Per fess   Per pale   Per bend   Paly   Barry   Bendy   Barry wavy

Quarterly   Per chevron   Checky   Pale wavy   Lozengy   Gyronny

Some charges:

Lion rampant   Fox sejant   Fleur de lys   Rose   Cross fleury   Axes in saltire (crossed)   Crescent

Choosing arms

The charges on coats of arms all have their own meanings. An escallop (shell) symbolized pilgrims and probably meant that the person who originally bore the arms had been on a pilgrimage. A bee might show someone who worked hard. A sword usually signified a soldier. Often, arms were a pun (play on words) on the bearer's name. The Spanish kingdom of *Castile* (Spanish for "castle") has a castle on its coat of arms.

This illustration, from a Spanish manuscript, shows the king of Castile (castle) and Leon (lion). On his arms, white has been used to represent silver. Heralds used white because silver would tarnish (darken in the air).

Blazoning a charge

It sounds like a term of war, but "blazoning a charge" is simply herald-speak for describing (blazoning) a coat of arms. Many of the terms come from ancient French. Descriptions begin with the field — whether it's a metal or color and how it's divided — before describing the charges upon it. Two made-up arms are shown below:

Vairy argent and vert
(Vairy is a stylized pattern of fur)

Per pale gules and azure, a galley (ship) or

In this castle scene, copied from a medieval illustration, the writer Christine de Pisan is presenting a book to Queen Isabel of Bavaria.

Castle life

In which you can find out exactly who was
who in a castle – who were the top dogs and
who looked after them. You can learn what
people ate, how they entertained themselves
and what life was like for the villagers
and townsfolk outside the castle walls.

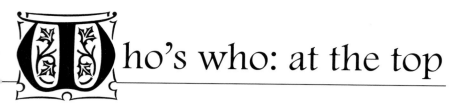

Who's who: at the top

King of the castle was the lord – or king. Everything revolved around him (or his wife if he was away). One of a lord's main tasks was visiting his estates and tenants, to check all was in order. (Which meant money owed to him was paid and no one was planning a revolt.)

When in residence, he chaired the local court, judging disputes and liberally handing out fines and punishments. He was also expected to host parties for visiting VIPs. But, busy as he was, a lord had to leave at a moment's notice if the king summoned him to Court or battle.

Seal of approval

In the early days of castles, a lord was too busy fighting to learn how to read and write. So, clerks wrote his letters for him. To prove they were from him, he sealed them with wax and stamped his mark with a seal.

The king's deputy

Many kings had a castle in each county. Since they couldn't be everywhere at once, they chose live-in officials to run them. The job of these officials was to raise taxes for the king and catch wrong-doers – so they weren't too popular with the locals.

The lord and his family relaxing in their solar

Seal of Isabella of Hainault

Seal of Robert Fitzwalter

My Lady

Titled women were under no illusions. Most were married for land not love. Being the lord's right-hand woman was no picnic. Even when her lord was there, the lady was in charge of the domestic side of castle life. When he was away, she was overall boss of the estates and defending the castle as well.

Her most important job was to make sure there was enough food and that the supplies in the storerooms matched the accounts. If guests were staying, she organized their sleeping quarters and entertainment. She also oversaw the upbringing of any children.

A tapestry

Wall painting

Granny rocking a grumpy baby to sleep

Playing with puppet knights

A game of chess

A medieval baby walker

Lady of leisure

In their limited spare time, ladies read, played board games, embroidered, sang or danced. For exercise, they rode or went hawking. If a fair was visiting, they could go on a shopping spree. There were also visits to friends, picnics, and trips to Court.

This picture, taken from a medieval manuscript called the Luttrell Psalter, shows a maid putting up her lady's hair.

 **Internet links**

Go to **www.usborne-quicklinks. com** for a link to a Web site about Warwick Castle in England. You can take a virtual tour inside its grounds and learn about the people who used to live in the castle.

Marriage

Marriages were arranged for children while they were babies and a girl was often married by 14. Her brother at 14 began to train as a squire, in the hope that one day he would become a knight.

A lady's work was never done...

Telling the House Steward to get rid of the smell in the Great Hall

Discussing a banquet menu with the House Steward and chief cook

Making sure the castle has enough cloth for clothes

Doctor, doctor

Many castles had their own doctor in residence. If not, the lady of the castle stood in. An expert on which herbs cured what, she supervised the growing of herbs in the garden and mixed the medicines herself.

Children

Any noble children running around a castle often belonged to the lord or lady's relatives. Nobles tended to trade children when they reached a certain age. This was as young as seven for boys, who were sent to relations to be pages. Girls were sent away to learn how to be a lord's wife.

Some toys: a hobby horse, a hoop and a ball

Toys were made of natural materials such as leather and wood.

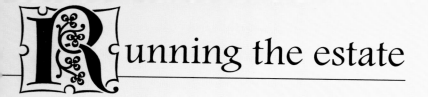

Running the estate

Even in the age of castles, lords had personal organizers — only they weren't electronic and they were known as stewards. Because most lords had several castles and numerous manors (estates of land) to command, not to mention royal and legal duties, they appointed stewards to run things day-to-day. Some had two stewards, one for their estates and one for the castle.

Stewards

The Estate Steward, helped by bailiffs, made sure the estates were run efficiently and that rents, fines and taxes were paid on time. As some rents were paid in food, this was vital. If the rent was owed from a manor several miles away, it was the Estate Steward who organized drivers and wagons to transport it.

Working closely alongside him was the House Steward. His main job was feeding everyone in the castle and he often had to plan a year ahead. If the storerooms weren't full in the fall, people would be hungry before the next harvest and they'd starve in a siege.

There was no supermarket to rely on either. If the cooks ran out of a luxury like sugar, the castle went without for several weeks, until the next fair came or they could visit the nearest town. Among his duties, the House Steward organized the salting of food to preserve it.

Hanging up hams to dry out

A servant carrying a sack of corn into the storeroom

Huge supplies of fish were brought in from the sea to be salted in the castle.

The House Steward overseeing the salting of fish

Because people grew bored with salted food, food was highly spiced. But spices were so expensive that the House Steward kept them under lock and key and rationed them. Apart from ensuring everyone ate, he was head of the Great Hall which meant finding and booking the entertainers to perform during banquets.

Clerks

The stewards were assisted by clerks. Being among the few in the castle who could read and write, the clerks were kept busy recording rents. Records of the lord's law courts also had to be kept. And if the lord was an official of the king, such as a sheriff, he would have to send regular reports to Court — not to mention friendly letters to keep in good with the king.

Almost every other day would see a missive sent to the royal household, congratulating the king on a princess's marriage or an enemy's death.

A portrait of Eadwine, a 12th century monk, stooped over his desk. Most clerks would have used a desk like this.

Putting the estates in order

Most lords had several manors – even if they only had one castle. Each manor had a manor house, occupied by a lesser lord or knight. These knights were helped by bailiffs, who oversaw the peasants' work and collected rents.

A bailiff and reeve

Under the bailiffs were reeves, elected by the peasants to guard their rights, represent their interests to the lord, and speak up for them in court.

The Chamberlain

The man in charge of the lord's chamber – his private rooms, money and valuables – was the Chamberlain, helped by the Treasurer. Since all money came into the castle as cash, and there were no banks, money was stored in a locked chest, in a guarded room. A strict record was kept of everything the lord owned, all the money paid in and every penny spent.

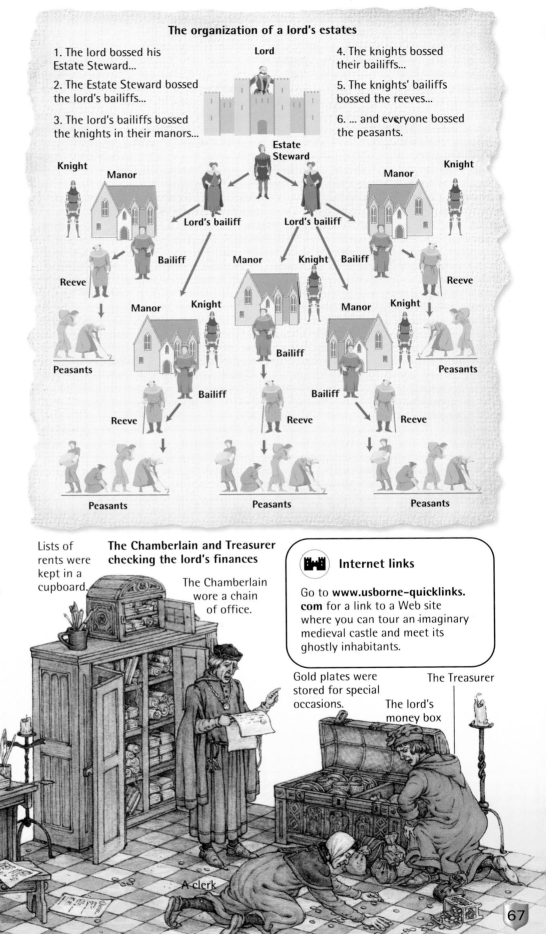

The organization of a lord's estates

1. The lord bossed his Estate Steward...

2. The Estate Steward bossed the lord's bailiffs...

3. The lord's bailiffs bossed the knights in their manors...

4. The knights bossed their bailiffs...

5. The knights' bailiffs bossed the reeves...

6. ... and everyone bossed the peasants.

Lord

Estate Steward

Knight

Manor

Lord's bailiff

Bailiff

Reeve

Peasants

Manor

Knight

Bailiff

Reeve

Peasants

Knight

Manor

Lord's bailiff

Bailiff

Reeve

Manor

Knight

Reeve

Peasants

Manor

Knight

Bailiff

Reeve

Peasants

The Chamberlain and Treasurer checking the lord's finances

Lists of rents were kept in a cupboard.

The Chamberlain wore a chain of office.

The clerk's desk, well-supplied with spare quills (feather pens)

A clerk

Gold plates were stored for special occasions.

The lord's money box

The Treasurer

Internet links

Go to **www.usborne-quicklinks.com** for a link to a Web site where you can tour an imaginary medieval castle and meet its ghostly inhabitants.

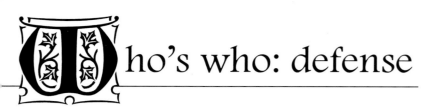

Who's who: defense

Castles needed guarding, even in peacetime, with rival lords always keen to expand their estate by taking over next door — by force if necessary. To make sure this didn't happen were the live-in fighters, under the Constable's command. These were men-at-arms and knights, who defended the castle in return for bed and board.

Most of the knights owned manors elsewhere, living in the castle for 40 days, as part of the rent owed to their lord. But sieges didn't stick to neat time limits and often knights were needed for more than 40 days at a time. So, eventually, they paid the lord cash instead. He then hired professional knights, who lived in the castle permanently.

Men-at-arms

Among the men-at-arms were archers, who used longbows or crossbows. Of course, in a crisis they'd use whichever weapon was handy. While the Constable gave them military orders, their immediate boss was a sergeant.

Watchmen

The soldiers kept a permanent watch from the battlements for approaching visitors, whether friend or foe. The lord also used soldiers as personal bodyguards, when he was out visiting. Robbers used to lie in wait for rich prey in the woods.

A surprise attack at sunset

A guard dozes while the enemy silently scales the walls.

This man-at-arms was distracted.

The Constable and guards race out to confront the enemy.

The soldiers have climbed the battlements to be challenged by some more attentive men-at-arms.

Internet links

Go to www.usborne-quicklinks. com for a link to a Web site where you can try out your Virtual archery skills. The archery test takes place in the Tower of London, so be warned: if your archery isn't up to it, you risk losing your head!

Pages and squires

Living in the castle with the knights was their entourage of squires and pages. Each page had certain duties within the castle, such as helping at mealtimes, though he was mainly there to learn.

Pages working on their weapon skills

Most of his day was taken up with lessons. First came reading, writing and Latin with a castle priest; then how to behave, including singing, dancing, and serving food – used to good effect during dinner. Pages also learned horseriding, and basic fighting skills using wooden swords.

At 14, a page became a squire and fought with a real sword. His schooling didn't stop, but now fencing lessons were more important than how to carve roast beef. He also looked after his knight's arms (weapons), held his horse and helped him prepare for battle. Being a trained fighter, a squire accompanied his knight everywhere – even into battle.

A pretend joust

The castle's Constable giving two pages a lesson in swordfighting

An older page takes aim at a target, riding a wooden horse pulled by two exhausted servants.

A squire's workout

Squires played sports to keep fit and agile and spent hours improving their fighting skills. They worked out at a quintain (see right) or by "Running the Ring." In this exercise, the squire rode past a row of small hoops and tried to spear them.

The quintain was a post with a spinning arm. It had a shield on one end and a weight on the other.

★

The squire rode up to the quintain from a distance, balancing his lance under his arm and aiming to hit the target squarely in the middle.

★

The quintain was a good test of a knight's coordination and reactions. If he didn't duck right away, he was whacked on the head.

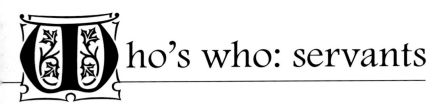

Depending on who was in residence, a castle was either crammed with people, or run by a small staff. As most castle owners owned more than one castle (in 1214, King John owned 100), they spent their time journeying between them.

Once all the supplies had been eaten — or the lady felt the castle needed a spring clean — they moved on to the next. Most servants went with them. The servants divided into two main groups: indoors and out.

Indoor staff

Some inside staff were attached to a certain room, the kitchen say, but others, such as the clerks, had a more general role. In the kitchen, there were four senior posts. The Pantler and Butler looked after food and drink. When the lord was in residence, food was bought, stored and eaten on a massive scale. The chief cook bossed dozens of undercooks and assistants in the kitchen, while the Ewerer was in charge of table linen.

Serving staff from a medieval manuscript called the Luttrell Psalter

Waiters and cleaners

The Great Hall had a separate team of serving staff to wait on the tables. Then there were ushers for every door and servants to repair clothes, air bedding, dust tapestries and replace the dirty rushes which covered the floors.

Weaving cloth at a loom, watched by a spider – a symbol of hard work

Lady's maids

On the whole, women were far outnumbered by men, though every castle had laundresses and several seamstresses who worked with the tailors. But, apart from nursemaids and a few female servants, the only other female residents were the family and ladies-in-waiting. These were relatives or other noblewomen who helped the lady with her day-to-day jobs. More importantly, they also kept her company.

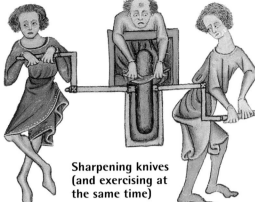

Sharpening knives (and exercising at the same time)

Handymen

Minor repairs were constantly needed, on anything from a rotten door to a leaking pipe. So, apart from skilled on-site craftsmen – the blacksmith and carpenter – there were always a few odd job men, and often a plumber, in residence.

Outdoors

The man responsible for everything that went on outside (except the weather) was the Marshall. He took charge of all outdoor staff, as well as activities such as hunting. He supervized any messengers running errands and carters making or returning with deliveries. He even kept an eye on all the castle's animals and birds.

But the Marshall's biggest headache came when his lord decided it was time to switch castles. A lord didn't just move his family, servants and a few clothes. He moved everything but the kitchen sink (which was stone and part of the wall). And his Marshall had to organize the packing of everything — from the lord's four-poster bed down to his silver spoons.

Internet links

Go to **www.usborne-quicklinks. com** for a link to a Web site where you can read an interview about life for lords and ladies – and their servants.

The lady's coach had blinds to protect against the dusty road.

The falconer calling back an escaped falcon

Carts were piled high with furniture.

Packing up a castle to move on to the next one involved everybody.

Sacks of pots and pans from the kitchen

Even the family pets had to be packed.

Food & feasting

The staples of everyone's diet were bread, cheese and vegetables. The castle gardens grew the vegetables, eaten fresh in season, and pickled or dried if not. Some castles had orchards. Northern ones grew apples and pears; those in the south grew grapes and citrus fruit. Castle owners kept bees too, as honey was used to sweeten food. Sugar came from the East and a small amount cost a year's wages.

Use your loaf

Since potatoes hadn't reached Europe and only the rich could afford rice, bread was served with every meal. Fine white flour was used for the lord's bread, coarser brown for the servants. Brown bread was also used for trenchers – slabs of bread used as plates (or fitted inside the silver dishes of the lord). At the end of each meal, these gravy-sodden crusts were given to the poor.

One man's meat

The wealthier you were, the better you ate, but living and working in a castle meant a fairly good diet for all. The lord and his highest officials ate the very best, such as venison after a hunt. Servants ate much plainer food, usually based upon a vegetable and barley stew, but they did get meat thrown in too.

Nobles ate meat – roasted or in pies – whenever they could, but the Church decreed that only fish could be eaten on certain days. To get around this, the Barnacle goose was described as a fish, just so it could be eaten on a "meat-free" day.

Stuffing a chicken

A banquet

One of a lord's duties was to be generous and lords frequently held banquets to impress and entertain visitors. On banquet days the menu grew exotic, with dishes such as peacock and swan. Food was even dyed to liven it up. The more important you were, the closer you sat to the lord's "top" table and the delicacies. At the lower ends of the tables, the food came along colder, plainer and later.

A banquet about to begin

Less important people sat further away from the top table.

A trencher

A meat pie

The minstrels warming up, ready to play when the feasting begins.

A page

Visiting entertainers were hired for the feast.

Stuffed peacock with its tail stuck back on

Count the cost

Banquets cost a fortune, but even the daily food bill was huge and the lord paid for it all. In 1275, for one meal, the household and two guests at Kenilworth Castle required three sheep, one and a half oxen, two kid goats, six hens and 300 eggs.

A guest Bishop saying grace before the meal

Chicken on a spit

The castle jester

The Chamberlain and Stewards

The Constable and his wife

The lord and his family sat at a table on a raised platform.

The "salt" (which held salt)

Mutton

The lord's mother

Beef stew

A castle made from marzipan

The lord's nephew, a page, taking a bowl of water to the top table for people to rinse their hands

Internet links

Go to www.usborne–quicklinks. com for a link to a Web site where you can see pictures of a life-size reconstruction of a banquet set in Enniskillen Castle, Ireland.

Fun & games

For the castle servants, life was all work and hardly any play. Lords and ladies, on the other (dripping with jewels) hand, had much more fun. Many lords kept a household jester — a live-in entertainment system — and for banquets, booked mime artists, jugglers, acrobats and singers.

On less raucous evenings, board games, gossip and embroidery kept everyone amused.

A fool from an illuminated letter

Gambling games played with dice were always popular. The fact that the church banned them (because people swore so badly when they lost) didn't stop anyone from playing.

Bored? Games

Some of the many board games included backgammon; "merrills", like noughts-and-crosses (tic-tac-toe); and "fox and geese", which was played like draughts (checkers). But for heart-stopping excitement, you chose chess. It could be fatal. One woman was stabbed by a bad loser; another man was battered with the board. He made the mistake of beating the king.

A woodcut of a man playing chess

Fair's fair

Servants did get some days off. No one worked on holy days (except priests) and after the church service, the day was theirs to feast, sing and dance. But they had most fun when the fair was in town, twice a year.

Fairs didn't have a giant slide, but almost as exciting were the foreign merchants with their exotic goods: spices from the East, wine from France and swords from Spain.

A lady choosing cloth for a new dress

Rolls of silk were brought from the Far East.

The town fair

A cheese stall

Fake medicine

Apple bobbing

A dancing bear

Sports

Sports included hockey, hammer throwing, swimming and bowling. Football was popular too, but with teams of up to 100-a-side, it was no fun being the referee.

Wrestlers entertaining the crowds

The sound of music

A medieval audience had two types of music: sacred (played in church) and "house" (played in the home). Early church music had no harmonies. Services were sung with a single tune – and not one you'd leave church humming.

Valuable goods were sold from a stall which could be locked up at night.

Street musicians played so people could dance.

Plays

Plays were first put on in church to teach peasants the Bible. These became morality tales, where good overcame evil. As their producer-vicars grew more ambitious, they were performed outside, where there was space for scenery and special effects.

A stall selling local produce, including honey

Polished silver mirrors

A puppet show

Internet links

Go to www.usborne-quicklinks.com for a link to a Web site where you can hear medieval music and play a game trying to guess what medieval instruments sounded like.

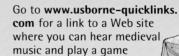

A priest shouting at a man selling relics such as angel feathers

Unloading a packhorse

Knives, ribbons and trinkets

A merchant selling jars of spices

Music & movement

Music played for fun was much livelier than church music. A band could be two people or a dozen, playing the hurdy-gurdy, viol, rebeck (3-stringed violin), flute, tambourine, lute, harp, organ, clarinet, cymbals, trumpet and drum. People danced in large circles, moving around in a stately fashion in time to the beat.

Wand'ring minstrels

Most musicians were permanently on tour. Singers called minstrels went from town to town, entertaining in castles if invited, otherwise performing in the street. Minstrels weren't only welcomed for their songs but their news.

Journeying around meant they brought gossip from other manors. But the stars of the day, who also toured but had more prestige than minstrels, were jongleurs. These singers could perform ballads of up to 30,000 lines from memory.

Minstrels accompanied themselves on lutes like this one, which were played a little like a modern guitar.

unting

Hunting wasn't just for the thrill of the chase. It was a way of putting fresh meat on the table, not to mention being an important social occasion. The day of a hunt began early, with a large breakfast for the lord and visiting nobles. Then, they saddled up and rode into the forest.

Peasants following the cart which carried any meat back to the castle

The hard work of tracking the quarry, whether boar, wolf, fox, bear or deer, was done by a huntsman and a couple of dogs. The huntsman told the lord which way to go. The lord blew a few rallying notes on his horn, which set off the hounds, and the chase was on.

A hunting party setting off

The lord leading the hunt

A decorated hunting cart from a medieval manuscript

Beaters

Some hunts used peasants to flush out animals, which dived for cover when a hunting party rode up. The peasants beat the undergrowth with large sticks, earning them the nickname "beaters". It meant a day out and almost a penny in wages.

The huntsman

A collar protected the dog's throat from a boar's tusks.

Royal forests

Most forest land was owned by the king, though lords were often granted hunting rights over any forests that surrounded their estates.

Stopping to pick up a beater who has tripped over a tree trunk

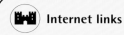 **Internet links**

Go to www.usborne-quicklinks. com for a link to a Web site which has pictures of dozens of hunting scenes taken from illuminated (illustrated) manuscripts.

A poacher running off before he is caught

Poaching

Lords were very protective of wildlife on their lands: only they had the right to kill it. If a villein tried, he wasn't hunting but poaching. Villeins were forbidden to kill any creature, even to protect their crops. But hungry peasants caught whatever they could, using bows and arrows, ferrets, nets and traps. Poachers faced severe penalties if they were caught, but it didn't stop them.

Sometimes the huntsmen stopped for a picnic on the way.

Taking a thorn from a dog's paw

The original sniffer dogs, trained to track down prey

Two outlaws taking cover – either on the run for wrongdoing or simply to escape their village

Hawking

Though very few ladies went hunting, everyone went a-hawking. This was a more gentle sport (except for the poor beast captured). Falcons were trained to fly from a noble's wrist to catch prey, either birds who flew too high for arrows, or smaller animals such as rabbits and hares.

An illustration of hawking from Les Très Riches Heures, a French manuscript

A modern French falconer dressed in medieval costume

Training a falcon

Falcons used in hawking were highly trained. Because training took time and care, falcons were very expensive and good trainers highly respected. In his book *The Art of Falconry*, Frederick II described the ideal falconer as small, patient, daring and even-tempered, with good eyes and ears.

The four stages of training

1. With its talons trimmed, eyes covered and bells on its feet, the falcon was carried around by the falconer.

2. The falcon took food from its master until it was half-tamed and used to being held by humans.

3. With its hood off but on a rein (creance), the bird flew after food on the end of a string (lure).

4. Finally the bird was taught to hunt. Flying free, it attacked small birds before returning to the falconer.

Pecking order

Just as there was a strict social order in everyday life, there were set rules as to who could hunt with which bird. Hunting with a gyrfalcon, if you were only a lord, would not go over well with the king. Lords were supposed to stick with peregrine falcons, while their wives made do with merlins.

Emperor:
Eagle

King:
Gyrfalcon

A falconer's kit

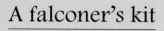
A lure attracted the falcon's attention.

A hood covered the bird's eyes and kept it calm.

A leash prevented the falcon from flying to freedom.

The padded glove stopped the falcon from biting the hand which fed it.

Bells helped the falconer to locate stray birds.

A leather purse held treats to reward birds who learned quickly.

Princes and lords:
Peregrine falcon

Baron:
Common buzzard

Knight:
Saker

Squire:
Lanner

Lady:
Female merlin

Free peasant:
Goshawk

Priest:
Sparrowhawk

Peasant:
Kestrel

A lady preparing to go hawking watched by the falconer

The falconer brought out birds from the castle on a portable perch.

Ladies rode sidesaddle

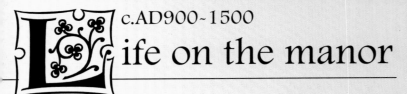

Life on the manor

A lord wasn't only responsible for his family and castle staff, but also for the peasants or villeins living and working in villages on his manors. Even by the end of the Middle Ages, almost 90% of the population of Europe were villagers.

The village

As no two castles were the same, so every village was different but most followed similar lines. Near the castle, and part and parcel of the lord's estate were a church, 20 or 30 huts for the villeins and a well or stream. There was also a mill and common-land for grazing cattle. Most important of all, were three vast fields. These grew the crops which fed the castle inhabitants and villagers – not to mention any besieging army on the rampage.

This shows the layout of a medieval village set in the middle of the three fields.

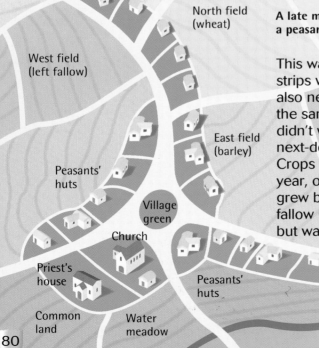

North field
(wheat)

West field
(left fallow)

Peasants'
huts

East field
(barley)

Village
green

Church

Priest's
house

Peasants'
huts

Common
land

Water
meadow

Open fields

The fields worked on the "open field" system. Each field was divided into numerous, narrow strips, separated by grassy paths. The villeins were allotted strips in each field, which were spread out so that good and bad land was evenly divided (though the lord had the best).

A late medieval woodcut showing a peasant sowing seeds by hand

This wasted time as a peasant's strips were a long way apart. It also needed everyone to put in the same effort. If one villein didn't weed his strips, the strips next-door were soon overgrown. Crops were also rotated. In any year, one field grew wheat, one grew barley and one was left fallow (empty). It rested the soil but was a huge waste of land.

A villein's lot

When they weren't needed to work on the lord's land (and he took priority, especially at harvest-time), villeins worked on their own. They followed the farming cycle. In the fall they plowed their strips, sowed seed, repaired tools and cleared ditches. Any animals which couldn't be fed during the winter were killed and their meat preserved.

A medieval scythe

Everything was done by hand, including harvesting crops with scythes.

In spring, oats, peas and beans were sown. Finally, after months of weeding, came the summer and harvesting the crops. While the sun shone, the villeins also made hay – literally – cutting and drying grass to see their livestock through winter.

Women grew vegetables and fruit and churned butter. They also made the family's clothes, spinning wool into a rough and ready thread. Even children did their share, looking after the animals and scaring birds from the crops.

Rent

All things came from the lord but the villein paid a high price for such generosity. In return for living on the lord's land and using his fields, villeins paid him a share of their crops, plus numerous other taxes.

They also paid in work, which usually averaged three days a week, farming his land. Other jobs included fetching a cartload of wood from the forest, lending him a couple of oxen for seven days a year, and washing and shearing his sheep.

Villeins used the lord's mill to grind their corn, his wine press to crush their grapes, and his oven to bake their bread: all for a fee. They even paid fines when a daughter married or if their son went to school.

A villein's hut with part of the wall cut away to show inside

Cooking was done over an open fire.

Vegetables were grown in a garden by the hut.

Home stuffy home

In the shadow of the lord's vast castle, sat the villeins' one- or two-roomed huts. Built around a wooden frame filled with wattle (twigs) and daub (clay), a villein, his wife, children and the family pig or goat all squashed in together. Their furniture was minimal – a table, a few stools and a chest. Even if the villein could afford a bed, few had room. Like the castle servants, people made do with straw mattresses on the floor.

A village on the lord's manor under the protection of his castle

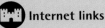 **Internet links**

Go to www.usborne-quicklinks.com for a link to a Web site where you can click on a wheel to find out more about the tasks in a medieval farmer's year.

The lord's mill

Woodpile

Geese

81

Crime & punishment

The Middle Ages are often thought of as a lawless time. This didn't mean there were no laws, as anyone who broke the king's or lord's laws could testify. But there was no national police force nor prison system — just the king's or lord's soldiers and royal or manorial justice.

The manor court

Serious criminals, such as murderers and thieves, were rounded up by the sheriff and tried by the king's judges (although occasionally a sheriff would take matters into his own hands). But the manor court — the lord in his castle — had authority over everything else.

For local disputes, the lord sat in judgement, pocketing the fines of anyone found guilty. If villein Y accused villein X of spreading lies about him, and X was found innocent, the lord could fine Y for wasting his time. Whatever happened, the lord was in pocket. A villein who didn't do his work on the lord's land, or trespassed in the lord's wood, was hauled before the manor court by the bailiff.

The reeve, as village spokesperson, pleading a villein's case with the lord

The manor court in session, with two opponents about to come to blows

Villeins who tired of being under the lord's control might try to run away. If they evaded capture for a year and a day, they were free men. The other villeins, however, had a duty to turn them in. In villages, where everyone was known, it was impossible to hide, so runaways fled to the towns.

Law of the town

Mayors and their councils took responsibility for wrong-doers in the town. During the day, they paid a constable to make arrests and keep law and order. At night, the "watch" took over. This was formed of citizens, who took turns to guard the town. Every town dweller, young and old alike, also had a duty to call out or make a "hue-and-cry", if they saw anyone committing an offense.

Offenders were swiftly brought before a court. They might be kept in a lock-up (cell) before the trial. But, if guilty, they were fined and flogged, not slung in prison.

A German "mask of shame" worn by men found guilty of a minor crime

Bells on the mask rang to let everyone know where the wearer was.

Internet links

Go to **www.usborne-quicklinks. com** for a link to a Web site about life in the Middle Ages. It was created by students and includes a quiz and a crossword puzzle.

A fit punishment

Humiliating people in public was thought the best way to punish them – and the best way to discourage others. So, gossips might face a dunking on the ducking stool.

The ducking stool

A butcher who sold bad meat might spend an afternoon in the pillory. He would be locked into its wooden frame, to face public ridicule and rotten fruit.

In this scene, two bakers are being punished for selling stale bread.

Punishments were often thought up to suit the crime. A nag could be put in a bridle. A seller of sour wine would have to drink some, then get the rest poured over his head. Serious offenders also faced a whipping. But murderers and even petty thieves were hanged, though treacherous noblemen could opt for beheading instead.

A jury of villeins sat alongside the judge in serious cases. Because the punishments for these were so savage, a jury often found someone innocent even when he or she was clearly guilty.

Proven innocent

In the early Middle Ages, old trial customs were still in place. If you could fight, you chose trial by combat: a fight to the death. There was also trial by ordeal, in which you might be made to carry a lump of hot iron for a few steps. If your hand healed within three days, you were considered innocent.

A German "mask of shame" worn by women found guilty of gossiping

Criminals were dragged through the village on a sled.

The pillory

Pelting the bakers with bad eggs and rotten vegetables

83

New towns & trade

Often, when a castle was built, a town grew up around it. Some, for example in Wales, were planned as a package, castle and town in one. Huge castle households needed a stream of supplies which a village alone couldn't meet. Castle owners also found that establishing a town was easy money as townspeople paid vast yearly rent for their land.

A town which has grown up around a castle, extending its walls

★

Who goes there?

Even towns which didn't share a castle's walls were often as well defended – with wall walks, battlements and towers for archers. Vast entrance gates were manned by guards twenty-four hours a day, seven days a week. Anyone coming in was often questioned first and at night the town was closed to all visitors until dawn.

Charter package

At first, towns were run by the lord – or his bailiff. But, as towns grew, merchants began to resent his control. Paying yet more money, they persuaded the lord to grant a charter letting them govern themselves. Headed by a mayor, councils were set up to run the towns: building and repairing roads, organizing defenses and managing fairs and markets. Some charters set up a town completely independent from the lord or king – creating city-states.

A wine merchant's boat

Town life

Towns were crowded, noisy, smelly and filthy, with garbage and sewage left to pile up in the street. It was the perfect place for disease. On the plus side, living in a town meant you had your freedom and possibly your own business.

Craftsmen lived in houses which were workshop and living quarters combined. Some craftsmen had shops in front of their workshops, selling ready-made goods, but most worked to order. They often stuck together, so all the bakers would be on one street, all the goldsmiths on another.

If you couldn't make anything, you could become a merchant, exporting goods and importing exotic foreign items such as spices and silks. For fresh food, there were weekly markets. People came in from the countryside to sell eggs, butter, cheese and organic fruit and vegetables. (Pesticides hadn't been invented yet.)

A street in a medieval town

Some roads were cobbled but most were dirt tracks with rain-filled potholes.

Many houses just had a hole in the roof to let out smoke.

Apprentices playing street football

Learning a trade

While a squire was learning the tricks of knighthood, the son of a craftsman was taught the tricks of a trade. Young boys were apprenticed to a master, living and sleeping in his shop. Apprentices worked hard and played hard too. Rowdy games of handball and street football helped to distract them from beatings and not enough food.

After seven years, a boy could become a "journeyman", free to do a day's work for anyone. The final stage was becoming a master craftsman in his own right, but this needed money. He also had to prove he was of a high enough standard, which he did by making an example of his work, called a "masterpiece".

Guilds (or Gilds)

To maintain standards and help fellow workers in difficulty, craftsmen began to form groups called guilds. The guilds made sure all work was of the highest quality, set fair prices and fined cheating tradesmen.

Members paid fees which were used to provide charity for sick colleagues (or their widows). The guilds also held feasts and provided annual entertainment when members put on religious plays. Later, rich merchants formed their own guilds and took over running the towns.

Internet links

Go to www.usborne-quicklinks.com for links to the following Web sites:
Web site 1 Take a tour of a Guildhall and find out about life as an apprentice
Web site 2 Play an adventure game set in a medieval town via a time machine

Ready cash

In the early days, money wasn't used much. People exchanged goods and services instead. But over time they began to buy and sell and pay wages in cash. Soon, lords needed money to pay for alterations to their castles and the luxury goods to go in them. As the demand for money grew, banks sprang up – to the fury of the Church, which didn't approve. Merchants grew wealthier, creating a new class of neither landowners nor villeins. It was the beginning of the end for the feudal system.

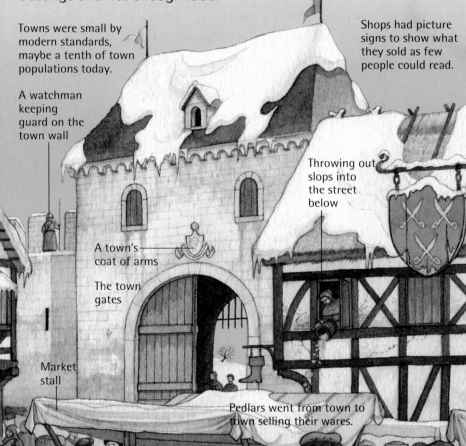

Towns were small by modern standards, maybe a tenth of town populations today.

A watchman keeping guard on the town wall

Shops had picture signs to show what they sold as few people could read.

Throwing out slops into the street below

A town's coat of arms

The town gates

Market stall

Pedlars went from town to town selling their wares.

The ruins of the crusader castle of Sidon in the Middle East

The beginning of the end

In which you will discover why castles were no longer built. You can also take a look at more recent castles and pick up tips for exploring ruins.
At the very end you'll find a timeline, showing changes in castle fashion, a glossary of castle terms, and a gazetteer listing some of the hundreds of castles in Europe, the Middle East and Japan.

Castles on the way out

Though castles were still being built in the late 15th century, by then in western Europe they were in decline. This was partly because the style of war had changed. Sieges cost so much time and money, it was better to fight it out on the battlefield.

Gunpowder was another factor but it didn't blow castles away at first. Early cannons were too temperamental and earthworks (ditches and banks) built in front of the castles absorbed any shock from cannon balls.

The main reason castles fell was the collapse of the feudal system, alongside the rise of nationalism (loyalty to your nation). As nobles lost power to the king, and stopped fighting over local plots of land, they didn't need the same level of protection from their homes.

Exploring castles

A medieval lord looking around his castle today would have a hard time recognizing it. Either it will be in ruins, or so altered it would seem like a different building. But there are always clues to help him (and you) reconstruct the castle that once stood there.

Entering the gatehouse, look for the tell-tale grooves on either wall, where the portcullis was winched up and down. Outside, you may see holes at the top of walls where hoardings once stuck out. And if the castle is surrounded by a muddy ditch, you've found the moat.

Doors and fireplaces sitting halfway up walls can show where floors were. Though the floors may have long since rotted, you can often see the square holes where ceiling joists once fitted.

Part of the ruined interior of Rochester Castle in Kent, England

Feudal system: R.I.P.

The feudal system was killed off by two things: fed-up people and fleas. Rulers didn't want reluctant knights fighting their battles, but a disciplined, regular army. Knights wanted full-time farmers on their estates, not resentful peasants with their own fields to plow. And the peasants wanted to be free.

Then, in 1347, fleas carrying the Black Death, hitched a ride to Europe on rats. In under three years, over a third of Europe's population died, most of them peasants. The few peasants who survived were suddenly in demand and rebelled. They wanted wages and if their lord didn't pay up, they moved on until they found a lord who would.

Corfe Castle in Dorset, England, was built in the 1080s as a motte and bailey castle on the side of this hill.

The keep, towers and curtain wall were added by various kings but destroyed in the English Civil War in the 1640s.

Henry's castles

By the time cannons were a force to be reckoned with, castles were becoming more home than fort. Besides which, the cannons needed to be housed in buildings with low, wide walls which were totally unsuitable for living in.

A diagram of a gun fort (fort for cannons)

Main entrance Keep

Inner curtain wall

Outer curtain wall

Ditch

Store rooms (below ground level)

Postern (back door)

★

Cannons need specialist gunners to operate them, too. So, new defenses were built for the guns and the soldiers who fired them. In the 1540s, Henry VIII built a series of gun forts along the English coast to guard against a threatened invasion. These were more like the ancient forts: castle building had come full-circle.

Internet links

Go to **www.usborne-quicklinks. com** for a link to a Web site all about Skipton Castle in Yorkshire, England, in the 1320s and today. You can print and make models of the gatehouse and kitchen, tour a 3D plan of the castle and view the photo gallery.

English Civil War

By and large, castles were left to rot or had their bricks plundered for new houses. But in England they briefly came into their own again in the 17th century, during the Civil War. The opposing teams of Cavaliers and Roundheads holed themselves up in castles, which saw lengthy sieges once more. Unluckily for the castles, the victorious Roundheads went around slighting (destroying) them, to prevent new uprisings from rebel Cavaliers.

Romantic castles

Two hundred years later, castles were popular again – but these owed more to fairy-tales than medieval fortified homes. King Ludwig II of Bavaria (or "Mad Ludwig", as he was known) emptied his treasury building castles. One of the most famous, Neuschwanstein, was built in 1869. The product of a set-designer's vivid imagination, it is now the blueprint for theme park palaces.

Neuschwanstein (New Swan Stone) Castle in the Bavarian mountains – so-called because nearly every room in the castle featured a swan in one form or another.

Timeline

950

From around the mid-10th century and throughout the Middle Ages, wars and skirmishes frequently broke out across Europe. Germany saw wars between rival emperors and states. In Italy, quarrels between emperors and popes also led to conflict, between the emperors' supporters (called *Ghibellines*) and supporters of the Popes (*Guelphs*). With fighting all around, the need for castles was overwhelming.

c950 Early castles are being built.

A lord and lady c.1000

1000

1000s
The feudal system is the basis of society.

The building of castles, including wooden mottes and baileys, spreads across Europe. Lords begin to build castles in stone.

Soldiers use huge, kite-shaped shields; chainmail is developed to protect them in battle.

Spanish hero Rodrigo Diaz de Bivar (*El Cid*), fights for and against the Moors in Spain.

1050

1066 Battle of Hastings: William, Duke of Normandy (in France), conquers England to become William I.

1073 The Saxons submit to Emperor Henry IV.

c.1078 William I builds the White Tower. One of the first stone keeps in England, it dominated London.

1083 Emperor Henry IV storms Rome.

1091 Conquest of Sicily by Norman adventurers completed.

1096-1099 The first of nine crusades is undertaken.

1100

1100s
Shell and stone keeps replace motte and bailey castles in England.

Chainmail body suits are worn.

1113 The Knights of St. John (the Hospitallers) founded to defend Christian kingdoms in the Holy Land.

1120 The Knights Templars founded.

1139 Civil war between Matilda and Stephen in England.

A lord and lady c.1100

1150

1150s
Stone castles built across Europe.

Surcoat worn over chainmail suit, often decorated with a knight's coat of arms.

1152 Henry II of England marries Eleanor of Aquitaine, gaining control over a large area of France. This leads to many wars.

c.1180 The start of polygonal keeps.

1190 Teutonic Knights founded.

A lord and lady c.1200

1200

c.1200 Round towers built.

Castle owners spread out into the bailey – keeps begin to fall out of fashion.

Round towers built at regular intervals in the curtain walls.

1204 Philip II of France takes Normandy from King John of England.

1226-38 Teutonic Knights conquer Prussia.

1245 The Pope declares Emperor Frederick II dethroned: war follows.

1250

Stone machicolations introduced.

c.1270 Gilbert de Clare builds Caerphilly, the first concentric castle in Britain.

1282 The Sicilians massacre their French rulers.

1291 Acre, the last Christian stronghold in Palestine, falls.

1292 Edward I of England intervenes in Scottish affairs, which begins over 200 years of hostilities.

1300

c.1300s

Metal plates worn over parts of the body on top of chainmail.

Castle designers begin to put comfort before defense.

1307-14 The Knights Templars are destroyed by the Pope and King Philip IV of France.

1309 Teutonic Knights make Marienburg their headquarters.

1310 Knights of St. John make Rhodes their headquarters.

c.1330 "Thunder tubes" invented.

1347-51 The Black Death sweeps Europe, killing a third of its people.

A lord and lady c.1300

1350

c.1350s on
The feudal system breaks down.

Castles built with the emphasis on comfort rather than defense; some are built of brick.

1337-1453 The 100 Years' War between France and England.

1370 Following the siege of the town of Limoges in France, Edward, the Black Prince (eldest son of Edward III of England), massacres the inhabitants.

1400

A lord and lady c.1400

c.1400s
Castle building in Europe declines.

Full suits of armor worn.

1410-11 Civil war in France.

1415 Henry V of England defeats the French at Agincourt.

1429 Jeanne d'Arc, a French peasant girl, ends the English siege of Orléans, France: two years later, after her capture and trial by the English, she is burned as a witch.

1442 Alfonso of Aragon conquers Naples in Italy.

1450

1457 The Poles take over Marienburg: the Teutonic Knights move to Konigsberg.

1485 Victory of Henry Tudor ends 30 years of civil war in England.

1492 Spain captures Granada from the Moors.

1494-5 France invades Italy and is driven back.

1498 Louis XII of France invades Italy and takes Milan.

1500

c.1540s
Henry VIII builds a series of gun forts along the coast of Britain.

1642-1649 English castles used and abused during the Civil War.

1869 on "Mad" Ludwig II builds his fairy tale castles in Bavaria.

A lord and lady c.1500

 Internet links

Go to **www.usborne-quicklinks. com** for links to Web sites where you can explore virtual castles alongside a timeline and check out a timeline of medieval technology.

Glossary & useful addresses

AD: "Anno Domini" (Year of the Lord); applies to years after the birth of Jesus

aketon: light padded jacket worn under *chainmail* to protect the wearer

almoner: person in charge of charity

apprentice: boy learning a trade

armor: protective clothing worn by *knights* in battle

arms: soldier's weapons; also see *coat of arms*

ashlar: name given to cut stone

bailey: area enclosed by defenses in which the castle buildings stood

barbican: extra-fortified gatehouse

battering ram: hefty pole with an iron tip, often hung on a frame and swung at walls to knock them down.

Battering ram

battlements: low wall at the edge of a roof (*parapet*) with gaps (*crenels*) and solid parts (*merlons*)

belfry: *see siege tower*

bow: weapon for shooting arrows with string tied to a curved piece of wood

  crossbow: bow fixed crossways to a piece of wood

  longbow: bow almost as tall as a man

Butler: person in charge of drinks

buttery: where the drinks in a castle were stored

buttress: stonework which sticks out from a wall to strengthen it

chainmail: iron rings linked together making a protective suit

Chainmail

chivalry: code of conduct followed by *knights*

coat of arms: emblem which decorated a knight's shield, so that he could be identified

Longbow

coat of plates: metal plates strung together and covered in material to make a tunic

concentric castle: castle with rings of walls, where the inner walls are higher than the outer ones

Concentric castle

Words in *italics* have their own entry in the glossary.

Constable: person in charge of security and the lord's deputy

courser: a hunting horse

crenel: gap in *battlements* through which missiles were fired

crenellate: to add *crenellations* or *battlements* to a castle

crenellations: *see battlements*

Crusade: war between Muslims and Christians (1096-1291)

crusader: European knight who fought Muslims for the Holy Land

curtain: wall around a castle

destrier: a lord's war horse

drawbridge: bridge which could be drawn up, to prevent attackers from entering

earthworks: banks and ditches built in front of a castle, to protect it from cannon fire

estate: a noble's share of land

Ewerer: person in charge of linen

falconer: person who trained the falcons used in *hawking*

farrier: blacksmith who shoes horses

feudal system: system of rights and obligations based on land

field: the background on a shield

forebuilding: entrance building on the front of a keep

gambeson: heavier, longer version of an *aketon*

garderobe: lavatory

gatehouse: tower with a gate to defend an entrance

gauntlet: glove

Great Hall: main room in a castle where people worked, ate and, early on, slept

Great Tower: *see keep*

guild (gild): group of craftsmen banded together to maintain standards

gun fort: fort for cannons

hackney: an inferior horse

hauberk: *chainmail* tunic

hawking: hunting small prey with birds, mainly falcons

Pike

helm: square helmet

herald: person who recognizes, designs and records coats of arms

Helm

heraldry: art of recognizing, designing and recording arms

hoarding: wooden gallery projecting from the top of a wall

joust: two *knights* trying to unseat each other with *lances*

keep: fortified building – the strongest place in a castle

  shell keep: *keep* with a circular stone wall around the motte. The castle buildings stood against the inside wall.

Shell keep

  square keep: square stone tower with a Great Hall on the first floor

knight: rich soldier on horseback

lance: long spear used by *knights*

loop or **loophole**: slit in wall to fire arrows or guns

machicolations:

(1) stone *hoardings*

(2) holes in the floor of the hoarding through which missiles were thrown

man-at-arms: footsoldier

mangonel: medieval catapult

manor: estate that supported a knight

Marshall: person in charge of outdoor activities and moving between castles

Master Mason: castle architect

merlon: solid part of *battlements* used by soldiers to hide behind

Merlon

metal: gold (or) and silver (argent) on a shield

meutrière: *see murder hole*

mews: shed which housed falcons

moat: ditch around a castle, sometimes filled with water

motte: dirt mound

motte and bailey castle: a castle, with a *keep* on a dirt mound, and other buildings surrounded by a wooden fence.

murder hole: hole in the roof of an entrance passage to drop missiles through, or pour water through to put out fires.

page: boy in the first stage of his *knight* training

Murder holes

palfrey: a horse used for everyday riding

palisade: wooden fence

Pantler: person in charge of food

parapet: low wall at the edge of a roof

pele (or **peel**) **tower**: mini version of a *keep*

pike: a long spear

portcullis: gate of wood and iron bars, raised to let people through a *gatehouse* or lowered to keep them out

postern: small side gate in a castle, used for secret raids on the enemy

putlog holes: holes left by scaffolding when building a castle

quintain: target used when practicing jousting

sally port: *see postern*

Siege tower

Samurai: Japanese *knight*

scullion: kitchen dogsbody

sentry: guard

siege: trapping inhabitants in a castle (or city) and trying to starve them out

siege tower: wooden tower used to reach the *battlements*

solar: the lord and his family's private bed-sitting room

sortie: surprise raid on an enemy

spur: spike on a *knight's* heel to spur on his horse

squire: *knight's* assistant; the next step to knighthood after being a *page*

Steward: a lord's personal assistant; important lords had two, one in charge of household affairs and one in charge of the estate

surcoat: cloth tunic worn over *chainmail*

tilt: fence dividing *knights* in a *joust*

tiltyard: area to practice jousting

tournament: pageant with jousting and sideshows

tower house: similar to a *pele tower* though often taller and sometimes L- or Z-shaped

tracing house: shed with a plaster floor on which windows and pillars were drawn to check their measurements

trebuchet: later version of a *mangonel*

Trebuchet before and after firing

troubadour: a knight-minstrel who composed and sang about heroic deeds done for love

undermine: to dig under a castle's foundations to bring it down

vair: a stylized version of the pattern made by squirrel furs when sewn together; always argent and azure

vairy: a form of vair with other colors and metals

Viking: person from Scandinavia

villein: peasant who worked for a lord in return for strips of land and the lord's protection

ward: *see bailey*

wardrobe: room off a lord's chamber for storing clothes; often where clerks worked, being one of the only quiet places in a castle

Movies

Movies can give you a very good idea of what it was like to live in a castle. Remember, though — many movies give an idealized (and cleaner) view. Some of the more realistic ones include:

• *Henry V* (either starring Laurence Olivier or Kenneth Branagh) especially for the battle scenes

• *Robin Hood, Prince of Thieves* which has some good scenes inside castles

• *El Cid* for a joust

• *The Lion in Winter* for life in a castle

Useful addresses

Some countries have national organizations dedicated to preserving and restoring castles. Many of these castles are open to the public.

In the UK:
English Heritage
PO Box 569
Swindon SN2 2YP

National Trust
36 Queen Anne's Gate
London SW1H 9AS

CADW
Welsh Historic Monuments
National Assembly for Wales
Cathays Park
Cardiff CF10 3NQ

Historic Scotland
Longmore House
Salisbury Place
Edinburgh EH9 1SH

For Irish castles, contact:
Dúchas the Heritage Service
7 Ely Place
Dublin 2

ap of castles in Europe

This map* shows just some of the many castles still standing in Europe. To list every castle in existence would fill the book and not begin to cover them all. The ones included here have either been mentioned earlier, were significant in their time or are some of the best surviving (or restored) examples.

On pages 96-97, there is a numbered list of all the castles shown on this map. To locate a castle, pick a flag number from the map and find it in the list, or turn the page and choose a castle, then check back to the map. Smaller maps, showing some of the castles in the Middle East and Japan, are on pages 98-99.

At first glance, the maps show you where a particular castle can be found. But, looking more closely, you can see how castles were built near rivers for the water supply, or to guard borders and coast lines. If you find a cluster of castles, the area was probably a trouble spot in the Middle Ages.

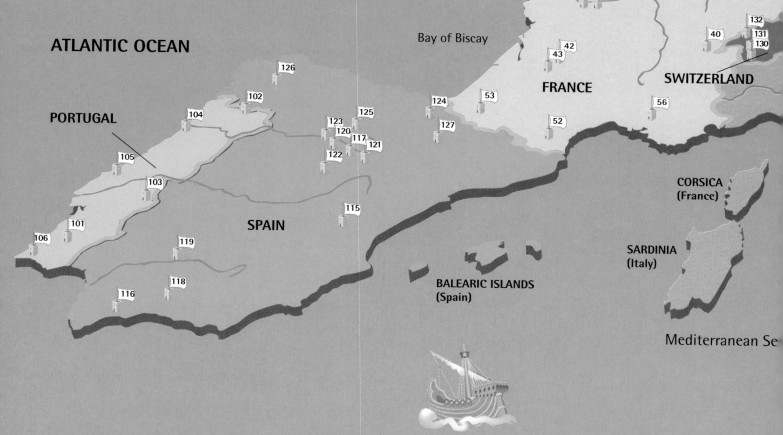

ATLANTIC OCEAN

ICELAND

SCOTLAND

North Sea

ENGLAND

IRELAND

WALES

NETHER-LANDS

BELGIUM

LUXEMBOURG

SWITZERLAND

Bay of Biscay

FRANCE

PORTUGAL

SPAIN

CORSICA (France)

SARDINIA (Italy)

BALEARIC ISLANDS (Spain)

Mediterranean Se

* Not to scale

ARCTIC OCEAN

Barents Sea

Norwegian Sea

FINLAND
38

97

NORWAY   SWEDEN

108

ESTONIA
90

DENMARK   128   Baltic Sea   LATVIA
16   17   129   91

15   RUSSIA   LITHUANIA

58   99 98   RUSSIA   BELARUS

GERMANY

67   61   73

65   POLAND
63 70 72   13

71   14   12   100   UKRAINE

69   64 57

60   2   CZECH REPUBLIC

68   1   SLOVAKIA   76

3   75

135   AUSTRIA   HUNGARY   MOLDOVA

84   89   6   4   5

83   88   114   ROMANIA

CROATIA   107

SLOVENIA   BOSNIA &
            HERZEGOVINA   Black Sea

YUGOSLAVIA   BULGARIA

86

ITALY   85 82   MACEDONIA   TURKEY

RUSSIA

ALBANIA

GREECE

SICILY   87

RHODES   74
(Greece)   CYPRUS

MALTA

CRETE

95

# Gazetteer: Europe

AUSTRIA
1 Dürnstein: now ruins on a cliff above the Danube, this is where Duke Leopold V of Austria held Richard I of England captive in 1192.

2 Festung Hohensaltzburg: a vast castle above Salzburg, started in 1077 and added to until the 17th c.*

3 Forchenstein: built in about 1300 to protect the border with Hungary. The keep survives from then.

4 Friesach: three castles, built in 1077, making up a fortified town.

5 Hochosterwitz: a castle with 14 gate-towers protecting its entrance.

6 Schloss Bruck

BELGIUM
7 Beersel: built in the 14th and 15th c. with moat and three corner towers.

8 Bouillon: owned by the Dukes of Bouillon, one of whom helped to lead the First Crusade.

9 Corroy-le-Château: built in the 13th c. with seven large towers.

10 Ghent: built on the site of a Viking fort in about 1180 and inspired by the crusader castles.

11 s'Gravensteen: a stone keep begun in 1180, surrounded by a wide moat and oval wall with 24 towers.

CZECH REPUBLIC
12 Hukvaldy: a ruined 13th c. stone castle which, unusually, was never adapted or rebuilt in later years.

13 Kalich: ruined castle of Jan Žižka, a Czech military leader.

14 Karlstejn: built in 1348 by Charles I of Hungary; rebuilt by Holy Roman Emperor Charles IV in the 15th c.

DENMARK
15 Hammershus: huge 13th c. castle with two baileys.

16 Nyborg: said to be Scandinavia's oldest royal castle, built in the 12th c. to protect the coast from pirates.

17 Vordingborg: the remains of a 14th c. castle, with two courtyards and the *Gaasetarnet* (Goose Tower).

ENGLAND
18 Alnwick: a motte and bailey castle fortified in stone in the 12th c. making a seven-towered shell keep.

19 Arundel

20 Bamburgh

21 Berkeley: a motte and two baileys converted into a shell keep; still owned by the Berkeley family.

22 Bodiam: *see page 30*

23 Conisbrough: a polygonal keep

24 Corfe: *see page 88*

25 Dover: royal castle built to defend the English channel coast.

26 Framlingham: *see page 16*

27 Kenilworth: vast 12th c. castle, with later additions.

28 Leeds

29 Orford: a polygonal keep

30 Oxford

31 Restormel: a shell keep

32 Richmond: a Norman castle said to have Britain's oldest Great Hall.

33 Rochester: one of the most impressive ruins in England, with a magnificent Great Hall.

34 Tower of London: built by William I, around 1087; its square keep is known as the White Tower.

35 Warkworth: a star-shaped keep dating from 1400.

36 Warwick: founded in 1068 but added to over the centuries; still home to the earls of Warwick.

37 Windsor: royal castle, one of the homes of the present queen.

FINLAND
38 Hame: an almost entirely brick-built castle, begun in the 1290s as a defense against Russian advances.

FRANCE
39 Angers: 13th c. castle with 17 round towers in the curtain wall.

40 Annecy: begun in the 12th c. but added to until the 16th c.

41 Arques-la-Bataille: first built in 1038; besieged by William I in 1052-3. Rebuilt by English king, Henry I, in the 1120s, it passed from the English to the French and back over the centuries.

42 Bannes: a mass of pointed roofs and towers, its mix of styles shows the design shift to comfort from defense.

43 Bonaguil: a 13th c. castle sited on a rocky outcrop between two valleys, with a pentagonal keep and round corner towers.

44 Caen: built by William I in 1050.

45 Château Gaillard: built by Richard I of England, now ruined; once one of France's finest castles.

46 Chinon: actually three castles in a row, linked by a moat.

47 Domfront: 12th c. ruins

48 Falaise

49 Fougères: an important military post with 13 towers, begun in the 12th c. The town grew up around it.

50 Gisors: ruins with polygonal keep.

51 Loches: a 12th c. keep, with remnants of 11th c. building work.

52 Montségur: built in 1204 with five sides and a huge square keep; destroyed after a two-month siege.

53 Pau: built near the Spanish border to guard a ford across a river; the birthplace of Henry IV of France.

54 Provins: a 12th c. keep known as the Tour de César; rectangular at its base, becoming octagonal higher up.

55 Saumur: the fairy-tale castle in *Les Très Riches Heures*, a medieval book written for the Duc de Berry.

56 Tarascon

GERMANY
57 Altenburg: begun in 1109 and home to the Bishops of Bamburg for 300 years, it was destroyed by fire in an attack in 1553; now restored.

58 Bentheim: the largest in Lower Saxony, built in 1116. The keep's base wall is almost 5m (16.4 ft) thick. One of the few castles that actually had a torture chamber.

59 Burg Eltz

60 Burghausen: built on a ridge, with six baileys divided by ditches.

61 Erfurt: *see page 30*

62 Gutenfels und Pfalz

63 Henneburg: now ruined, a semi-circular castle.

64 Kaiserburg: set on a ridge, one tower was built by Emperor Henry III.

65 Lichtenstein: built in the 13th c. and rebuilt in the 19th.

66 Marksburg: built on the Rhine, around the beginning of the 13th c. with a triangular courtyard.

67 Münzenburg: a 12th c. castle with oval bailey.

68 Neuschwanstein: *see page 89*

69 Rothenburg

70 Sterrenburg & Liebenstein: two castles built side by side, divided by a wall and moat, supposedly by two nobles in love with the same lady.

71 Thurant: a double castle with twin towers.

72 Wartburg: built of wood in the 11th c.; rebuilt in stone in the 12th. Martin Luther stayed here while translating the Bible into German.

*Throughout the gazetteer, c. is used as an abbreviation for century.

73 Wildenburg

GREECE
74 Rhodes: built by the Knights Hospitallers, a group of Christian knights, in the early 13th c.

HUNGARY
75 Esztergom: built on the Danube, an important site since Roman times, the castle dates back to the 10th c.

76 Sarospatak: first built in the 12th c. to protect the Bodrog valley and enlarged a century later.

IRELAND
77 Blarney: a stone castle built in 1210. The "Blarney stone" (said to give eloquence to those who kiss it), rests on the battlements.

78 Cahir: one of Ireland's largest and best-preserved castles. The staircase inside one of the towers leads to the river so inhabitants could get water during a siege.

79 Carrickfergus: built in 1180, the first for an Anglo-Norman lord.

80 Roscommon: a rectangular-ward with twin-towered gatehouse.

81 Trim: a keep in a triangular ward.

ITALY
82 Bari: a square keep enclosed by four huge square stone towers.

83 Buonconsiglio: built in 1239-1255, its massive round Augustus Tower may date from Roman times.

84 Caldes

85 Castel del Monte: *see page 32*

86 Castel Sant'Angelo

87 Castello Ursino (Sicily): a square castle with round towers, built in 1239 and later adapted.

88 Stenico: started in 1163; a mix of styles up to the 15th c. when converted into a comfortable home.

89 Toblino: set on an island, with a tower and living quarters at one end.

LATVIA
90 Riga: a vast rectangular castle built by the Teutonic Knights.

LITHUANIA
91 Trakai: set centrally in a series of lakes, the castle (keep and three round towers) dates from the 14th c.

LUXEMBOURG
92 Vianden: one of Europe's largest castles, today's remains date from the 13th and 14th c. Its Great Hall (the Knight's Hall) held 500 people.

NETHERLANDS
93 Doornenburg: a brick castle with parts dating back to the 13th c.

94 Muiderslot: built on a site in use since 1000.

95 Radboud: a huge castle built in the 13th c. on the site of an earlier fort. Mostly demolished by the 19th c.

96 Rozendall: brick castle with walls 4m (13ft) thick.

NORWAY
97 Akershus: a palace-castle, adapted over the years, with original 14th c. walls at its center; an official royal residence today.

POLAND
98 Marienburg: a rectangular brick castle; HQ of the Teutonic Knights.

99 Marienwerder: 14th c. castle built by the Teutonic Knights.

100 Wawel: sited at Krakow, replacing an 8th c. wooden castle. During 14th c. alterations, a cathedral was built inside it.

PORTUGAL
101 Beja: built on the site of a Roman fort and much altered.

102 Braganza: a square keep built by King Sancho I of Portugal in 1187 to protect Portugal against Spain.

103 Elvas: the largest square keep in Portugal, originally built by the Moors but captured by Sancho II in 1226, when it was altered.

104 Guimaraes: a 15th c. castle with a keep built from the tower of the previous castle on the site.

105 Leiria: a castle-palace with huge square keep.

106 Silves: first built by the Moors; rebuilt and expanded by Christians and restored in the 20th c.

ROMANIA
107 Bran: a 13th c. wooden castle built to guard the city of Sibiu. Rebuilt in stone in 1377; said to be the setting for the 19th c. novel *Dracula*.

RUSSIA
108 Novgorod: built by King Yaroslav in 1044, the oldest surviving castle-fortress in Russia.

SCOTLAND
109 Caerlaverock: a triangular castle with twin-towered gatehouse.

110 Craigievar: *see page 33*

111 Edinburgh: built on a rocky crag, the home of the Scottish kings.

112 Stirling: built at the entrance to the highlands, passing from Scottish to English hands and back.

113 Tantallon: built of pink stone overlooking the North Sea in the late 1300s; abandoned in the 17th c.

SLOVENIA
114 Bled: built on a hill in the 11th c. to guard the lake and town of Bled.

SPAIN
115 Alarcon: first built by the Moors and now used as a hotel.

116 Alcazaba (Malaga): Moorish castle on a hill linked to another castle by zigzagging walls.

117 Alcázar (Segovia): *see page 44*

118 Alhambra (Granada): dating from the 13th c. its designers used the natural defenses of a high ridge.

119 Banos de la Encina: built by the Moors in 967-968, with 15 towers in the curtain wall and a stone gateway shaped like a double-horseshoe.

120 Coca: a brick palace-fortress, built for the Archbishop of Seville.

121 El Real de Manzaneres: *see page 17*

122 Escalona: one of Spain's largest castles, first built by the Moors in the 10th and 11th c. Built of stone bonded with lines of bricks, typical of its *mudejar* (Moors under Christian rule) builders.

123 La Mota: *see page 32*

124 Olite: a wedge-shaped castle-palace built in the 15th c. with baths, roof gardens and even a small zoo.

125 Penafiel: a long, narrow castle.

126 Ponferrada: granted to the Knights Templar in 1185, their new castle on this site protected pilgrims.

127 Sadaba: built on the frontier between Christian and Muslim Spain, in the early 13th c.

SWEDEN
128 Hälsingborg: first built by the Danes on a narrow strait (when they ruled both sides) and rebuilt in 1370 with walls nearly 4.6m (15ft) thick.

129 Kalmar: dating from the late 13th c. with circular wall, four round towers, two gatehouses and keep.

SWITZERLAND
130 Aigle: a 15th c. castle with huge keep, first built in the 11th c.

131 Chillon: *see page 33*

132 Grandson: a vast 13th c. castle, with high walls and round towers.

133 Hapsburg: adapted over many centuries, originally the home of the Hapsburg dynasty.

134 Kyburg: dating from 1200, the chapel has 15th c. wall paintings.

135 Tarasp: dating back to the 11th c., the castle is still lived in today.

WALES
136 Aberystwyth: *see page 28*

137 Beaumaris: *see page 28*

138 Caernarfon: a motte and bailey castle built in 1090; rebuilt in stone by Edward I of England, 1283-1330, who intended it as his Welsh HQ.

139 Caerphilly: *see pages 28-9*

140 Harlech: *see page 28*

141 Pembroke: a round keep

142 Rhuddlan: *see page 28*

JAPAN

1 Edo Castle: built in 1457 in Edo (Tokyo) before it had become a major city, the main keep was destroyed 200 years later in a fire and not replaced. Japan's present emperor and his family live in part of Edo-jo today, in the Imperial Palace.

2 Hamamatsu (Hikuma-jo): first built in 1570 and expanded in 1577, the curtain wall still dates back to 1577, though the keep has been reconstructed.

3 Hikone: taking nearly 20 years to build, parts of the castle were taken from others nearby which had to be demolished under Japan's "one castle in each province" rule.

4 Himeji*: begun in the mid-14th c. but not completed until 1609, its thick walls were built to withstand rebellious warlords and earthquakes.

5 Hirosaki (Takaoka-jo): a three-floor keep built in 1810 to replace the five-floored keep of 1611 which burned down less than 20 years after being built, when lightning struck it.

6 Hiroshima: a reconstruction of the castle built by a powerful *daimyo* in the 1590s and destroyed by the atomic bomb during World War II.

7 Inuyama (Hakutei-jo): built in 1537; still owned by the family who took it over in the 1600s.

8 Kakegawa (Kumokiri-jo): built in 1513 and renovated at the end of the 16th c., the keep was rebuilt using traditional building methods.

9 Kumamoto: built in 1600, but largely burned down during a siege. One of the corner towers, which looks like a keep, may be the very first keep which was later replaced. Unusually, the roof gables follow straight rather than curved lines.

10 Nihonmatsu: made up of two castles, at the top and bottom of a hill, the first was built at the end of the 14th c.; the second in the mid-1580s.

11 Osaka (Kin-jo): built in 1583 and captured in 1615, despite its strong fortifications. In 1620, the new owners rebuilt on a larger scale, but it burned down after being struck by lightning.

12 Wakamatsu (Kurokawa-jo): first built in 1384, today's keep dates from the 16th c.

ARCTIC OCEAN

HOKKAIDO

HONSHU

JAPAN

Sea of Japan

SHIKOKU

KYUSHU

East China Sea

PACIFIC OCEAN

* See page 53